CHRISTOPHER LEHMAN & K[...]

Falling
in Love
with Close
Reading

Lessons for Analyzing Texts—and *life*

Foreword by **DONALYN MILLER**

HEINEMANN
Portsmouth, NH

Heinemann
361 Hanover Street
Portsmouth, NH 03801–3912
www.heinemann.com

Offices and agents throughout the world

The authors and publisher wish to thank those who have generously given permission to reprint borrowed material:

Excerpts from Common Core State Standards © Copyright 2010. National Governors Association Center for Best Practices and Council of Chief State School Officers. All rights reserved.

Acknowledgments for borrowed material continue on page iv.

Library of Congress Cataloging-in-Publication Data
Lehman, Christopher.
    Falling in love with close reading : lessons for analyzing texts and life / Christopher Lehman and Kate Roberts.
        pages   cm
    Includes bibliographical references.
    ISBN 978-0-325-05084-3
    1. Literature—Study and teaching (Secondary). 2. Language arts (Secondary). I. Roberts, Kate. II. Title.
    LB1631.L347 2013
    807.12—dc23   2013022680

Editor: Tobey Antao
Production: Hilary Zusman
Cover and interior design: Monica Ann Crigler
Typesetter: Kim Arney
Manufacturing: Steve Bernier

Printed in the United States of America on acid-free paper
17   16   15   14   EBM   4   5

Contents

Foreword

The first book I fell in love with was *The Velveteen Rabbit*, Margery Williams' tender story about a stuffed rabbit whose owner loves him so much that the toy becomes real. I read and reread my copy until the pages wore down and the spine split. Eventually, I didn't need the book anymore—committing so many lines to memory that I could revisit the little rabbit whenever I wanted. Even now, 40 years later, I can call up the Skin Horse's explanation of how you become real:

> *"Real isn't how you are made," said the Skin Horse. "It's a thing that happens to you. When a child loves you for a long, long time, not just to play with, but REALLY loves you, then you become Real."*
> *"Does it hurt?" asked the Rabbit.*
> *"Sometimes," said the Skin Horse, for he was always truthful. "When you are Real you don't mind being hurt."*

Although I read many books when I was small, *The Velveteen Rabbit* was the first book I read that I felt was telling me something important. The first book that evoked tears. The first book that became a part of me, and remains a part of me still.

We never forget our first love. Thankfully, no one thinks you're fickle or wanton if you fall in love with book after book. I have loved scores of books over my long reading life and each one holds memories that remain forever linked to what I read. Inspired by Laura Ingalls Wilder's Little House books, my sisters and I played homestead in our backyard—harvesting crops and tying our St. Bernard to our wagon. Bennie wasn't convinced he was an ox, but we were. We named the orb weaver who lived over our kitchen screen door Charlotte. I watched her weave for hours. She never spelled a word, but the bold zipper stripe she stitched down her web every night fascinated me.

I collected book friends throughout my childhood—Paddington Bear, Henry and Beezus, Meg and Charles Wallace, Mowgli, and many others. Endless hours sailing pirate ships and taming unicorns, new words like *periwinkle* and *metamorphosis* tasted and saved for later, libraries plundered and dark forests crossed—my childhood was richer because I loved to read.

Although I left my childhood decades ago, it never left me. I can still visit my ten-year-old self every time I open *Black Beauty* or *The Borrowers*. As Oliver Wendell Holmes, Sr. said,

"Where we love is home. Home that the feet may leave, but not our hearts." Every book I read provides another place for my heart to reside, another home, and I am grateful for it.

As a teacher, I expect my students to read widely, explore what written language offers, and build capacity for reading by analyzing, evaluating, and discussing lots of texts. I also want my students to find reading enjoyable and meaningful throughout their lives—to love reading. There is some debate about whether we can teach students to love reading at all. According to Alan Jacobs, Distinguished Professor of Humanities at Baylor College, you can't. In his book *The Pleasure of Reading in an Age of Distraction* (2011), Jacobs claims that "the idea that many teachers hold today, that one of the purposes of education is to teach students to love reading—or at least appreciate and enjoy whole books—is largely alien to the history of education. And perhaps alien to the history of reading as well." Our sole charge, many educators claim, is to ensure that our students possess the literacy skills needed to succeed in the workforce. It's vital that students graduate from high school with the reading skills they need for college and career success, but I want more for them. I hope our students find relevance in their lives, forge deep connections with others, create art, appreciate the world's mysteries, and possess spiritual and emotional stores that sustain them in dark times. Reading shows us how to be better human beings, not just successful worker bees.

Teaching students how to read well and helping them discover a love for reading aren't disparate goals. I believe we must guide students toward both. As teachers around the country work to implement Common Core State Standards in their schools, however, many express increasing concern about changes in reading instruction that dismiss students' aesthetic connections and engagement with what they read. CCSS emphasize close reading—the reading, rereading, and analysis of text for the purpose of interpreting it. Teaching students to examine texts deeply, evaluate author's craft and purpose, and develop an understanding of greater themes and ideas are important reading skills that students need in order to comprehend and appreciate text.

Unfortunately, because of limited training and misinterpretation of the new standards, many administrators and teachers have an inconsistent, incomplete, or incorrect understanding of what close reading is, how to teach it, or how close reading can fit into research-proven reading pedagogy.

As I travel the country working with teachers, many feel that their entire reading program must shift to endless close reading events using difficult texts. Once confident teachers now feel inadequately prepared to teach reading. Rushed to realign instruction with CCSS, teachers feel pressure to abandon independent reading, read alouds, comprehension strategy work, and other instructional components proven to increase students' reading confidence and competence. We cannot throw out what we know our students need. We must develop reasonable, functional tools for teaching close reading that align with best practices. Students deserve instruction that moves them forward as readers and thinkers and values their unique experiences and needs.

Finding this balance is not impossible. We can teach our students how to read closely and fall in love with reading. Chris Lehman and Kate Roberts are lighting the way with *Falling in Love with Close Reading*. Smart educators who care about students and teachers, Chris and Kate offer a practical, manageable framework for teaching students how to read closely. Using lenses to focus readers' examination on one element of text such as characterization, word choice, or text structure, students collect information about what they read. Looking for patterns in a text, students evaluate the choices writers make and develop a deeper understanding of the text and its greater message. This sequence of lenses to patterns to understanding will be easy for teachers to use with a wide range of reading materials and a diverse group of learners. Simple. Effective. Adaptable. Brilliant.

Students will be able to practice and internalize this close reading sequence until it becomes a habit they can use forever—not just in English class. Kate and Chris understand how readers read. They know that artificial school-based reading tricks and tools don't help students become better readers over the long run. You won't find any gimmicks, acronyms, or special organizers here. You won't find laborious activities that crowd out meaningful reading, writing, and discourse, either. Kate and Chris know that students must spend most of their time reading—not filling out worksheets and answering questions. Throughout this book, you will find instructional moves and rituals that really teach our students how to read better and find greater appreciation and enjoyment for what they read. Instead of narrowing our students' reading lives to the boundaries of a page, Chris Lehman and Kate Roberts have liberated our students (and us).

Falling in Love with Close Reading, a resource-rich book, includes lesson plans, guiding questions, relevant texts that relate to our students' lives, and authentic examples that reveal students' thinking and development.

Beyond teaching our students how to read critically and effectively, Kate and Chris show how close reading skills transfer into life skills that help students navigate personal challenges and relationships. How does examining an author's point of view help students develop empathy for a friend's point of view? How does evaluating text structure help students evaluate the structure of their daily routines? Kate and Chris build relevance into every lesson—showing students that learning to read texts well helps them learn to read the world.

Through their sense of humor, wise advice, and positive message about teaching, Kate and Chris show their respect and regard for students and teachers every step of the way. They are teachers at heart. You know it from the first paragraph. They understand our challenges and share our passion. They know what it's like to work with a wide range of student abilities and interests. And they anticipate and provide the suggestions and resources we need to extend or reteach students who need something more.

Whether you need a guide that leads you through a school year of close reading instruction or a menu of ideas that enhance your current teaching, *Falling in Love with Close Reading* is what you've been looking for. Follow Chris and Kate and the students in this book through a journey of learning and joy. I am a better teacher for reading this book. My students will be better readers because of what Chris and Kate taught me here.

We can never lose sight of our true purpose: teaching our students to love reading so much that it becomes real to them—forever. Unlike *The Velveteen Rabbit*, becoming a real reader should never hurt.

—Donalyn Miller
July 2013

Acknowledgments

Every word of this book was formed through the generosity of countless educators. Within the fibers of these pages we see your faces, your students, and your talents.

Deep gratitude to the educators who offered their time, classrooms, and brilliant students to pilot, question, revise, and shape our thinking. In particular we want to thank Anne Bennet, Maureen Cassarino, Lauren Cohen, Claudia Crase, Lisa DiNatale, Ryan Dunbar, Sarah Mulhern Gross, Amanda Hecker, Molly Magan, Rebecca Masella, Connie Miller, Sarah Reedy, Heather Rocco, Rachel Smith, Brian Sweeney, and Carrie Tenebrini for your support of this book.

We also owe an incalculable debt of gratitude to the teachers, coaches, administrators, schools, and organizations that have been workshops for our thinking and inspirations for our teaching: Intermediate School 230, AIS Vienna, Carroll Gardens School for Innovation MS 442, The Laboratory School of Finance and Technology MS 223, ACORN Community High School, Taipei American School, E. M. Baker Elementary, Junior High School 67, East Ridge Middle School, Great Neck North Middle School, Our World Neighborhood Middle School, Woodward Parkway Elementary, Burnet Hill Elementary, Union County Public Schools, National Council of Teachers of English, International Reading Association, The Nerdy Book Club, All Write Consortium, Public School 19, Bay Lane Middle School, St. HOPE Leadership Academy, Oyster Bay High School, and the education community (and friendships) on Twitter.

Our ears have been tuned and eyes focused most by the mentoring and example of Lucy Calkins and our colleagues and friends from the Reading and Writing Project at Teachers College, Columbia University. We have been raised in the tradition of respecting children's voices and reflecting on adolescents' needs, believing deeply in the power of education and the thoughtfulness of professional educators. Lucy has helped us see the power in every person's literacy and find strength in our own voices as well. For all of this we are grateful beyond words. Additional thanks to those who read early drafts of this book and offered thoughtful feedback: Brooke Geller, Audra Robb, Emily Strang-Campbell, Annie Taranto, Kathleen Tolan, and Mary Ehrenworth. You gave us a hoist over the fence when we needed it most. A special thank-you to Maggie Beattie Roberts who first whispered, "This feels like a ritual"— your seemingly small insight grew the heart of this book exponentially.

To our champion and star, Tobey Antao, "editor" is only one hat you wear. You are a friend, cheerleader, evangelist of teachers and children, and passionate advocate for education. This book is as much yours as ours, you are in every page.

We feel lucky to have the talents of the Heinemann family along for this journey. To the entire editorial team for your "what if . . ." thinking that led us down paths we had not realized were in us. Thank you Sarah Fournier, Hilary Zusman, Patty Adams, Suzanne Heiser, and Lisa Fowler for the magic you create. Monica Crigler, a heartfelt high five for a stunning design. Elisia Brodeur, thanks for your careful eye and magical control of language. We appreciate Eric Chalek for every single thing, including a discussion of the power and nuance of an em dash. Cathy Brophy, Maureen Foster, Michelle Flynn, and your team, we are honored by your belief and support. Lesa Scott and Vicki Boyd, we are in awe of your boundless vision.

Finally, the ancients spoke of having a muse—a source of energy, a force that allows for creation. We could not have written this book without our muses, Yesenia and Maggie. It is not only that you supported us with long hours of writing time, constant encouragement, and much needed breaks (to play trains with Marcos or snuggle up with Hutch), it is that without *you*, there would be no *us*. You are the reason we are as we are now and a huge part of why this book exists. Thank you, Yesenia; thank you, Maggie—our inspiration, our fallen-in-loves.

Close Reading, A Love Story

The unexamined life is not worth living.

—Socrates

Think of what you love most in the world: your children, spouse, family, and friends. Your home or a memento from a vacation. Your cat. That old sweater you have had forever. Now consider how well, how intimately, you know those things. How when your partner has a certain look on her face, you know she is feeling sweet on you. How, on lucky occasions, you can preempt your child's tantrum. How every thread on that sweater is as familiar as the fingers on your hands. Think of the first person you fell in love with. Think of the last.

We know, in our bones, that loving something or someone involves knowing that thing or person very well. Returning to it repeatedly, gazing at it for hours, considering each angle, each word, and thinking about its meaning.

Our connection to the written word can be as deep as a love affair. Think of those books, the ones you memorized every line of when you were young, like "In the light of the moon a little egg lay on a leaf," you said over and over as a hungry caterpillar was just about to hatch, or "Goodnight stars, goodnight air, goodnight noises everywhere" filled your thoughts as a busy room, a moon, and *you* lay down for sleep (Carle 1979; Brown 1947). Think of the young-adult novel you came to know so well that you wanted to rewrite the ending. The songs you listened to as a teenager that played on repeat in your head. The first movie you memorized every line of. The television drama you feel you nearly inhabit.

Love brings us in close, leads us to study the details of a thing, and asks us to return again and again. These are the motivations and ideas that built this book. In it, we argue that teaching readers to look at texts closely—by showing them how one word, one scene, or one idea matters—is an opportunity to extend a love affair with reading. It is also a chance to carry close reading habits beyond the page, to remind students that their lives are rich with significance, ready to be examined, reflected upon, and appreciated.

What Close Reading Was, Is, and Can Be

Close reading developed from exactly this same place of deep love and study. It brings to mind ancient images of monks and scholars pouring over religious writings to try to divine an understanding of life's mysteries. The term *close reading* draws its roots from a passion for talking and writing about texts.

As university students of literary criticism in the 1940s aimed to develop ways of studying texts and engaging in thoughtful conversations, professors took to studying and detailing methods of teaching these analytical skills. This all ignited an academic debate, as so often happens. Scholars began to discuss the *best* approaches for talking about the literature they studied. One style that emerged, "New Criticism," argued that if you were going to talk about text, the conversation should be *only* about the text, not the time period, the author, or the reader's own experiences or points of view (Ransom 1941; Wimsatt and Beardsley 1946, 1949; Wimsatt 1954). Reading closely, then, was the process of trying to tune out everything else while looking at the style, words, meter, structure, and so on, of a piece of writing—letting the text itself shine through.

Other styles of literary critique developed alongside, from, and sometimes in opposition to, New Criticism. Several prominent approaches suggested that reading is an interaction between a particular reader and how that person sees the text—that it is impossible to remove experience from understanding. Others believed that considering the time period, or what was known of the author, were beneficial when discussing written works (Rosenblatt 1938,

1978; Fish 1970; Veeser 1989). In the late 1950s, the New Criticism style largely fell out of vogue at universities. Each approach, though varied in procedure and focus, involved reading closely and centered around the reader connecting deeply, intellectually, and passionately with making meaning from literature.

Today, the Common Core State Standards have brought the idea of close reading back into the educational landscape. As Lucy Calkins, Mary Ehrenworth, and Christopher Lehman describe in *Pathways to the Common Core* (2012), the Common Core State Standards' writers began with their vision of university reading and developed grade-level-specific expectations from there, meaning that the Standards across all grades inherently value "objective, close, analytical reading" and aim to move students in that direction. This careful meditation on texts is repeated throughout the language of the Standards:

- "read closely" and "cite specific textual evidence" (R.1)
- "analyze how . . . ideas develop and interact" (R.3)
- "interpret words and phrases" and "analyze how specific word choices shape meaning" (R.4)
- "analyze the structure of texts" (R.5)
- "assess how point of view" "shapes" a text (R.6)
- "analyze" "two or more texts" to build knowledge (R.9).

The CCSS even begins its introduction with a vision for students' potential at graduation, imagining that "students who meet the Standards readily undertake the close, attentive reading that is at the heart of understanding and enjoying complex works of literature" (p. 3).

Recently, the debate over New Criticism has been thrust back into the educational conversation after the adoption of the CCSS. Most likely this renewed focus came from the "Revised Publishers' Criteria" (2012), written by two of the lead writers of the standards, David Coleman and Susan Pimentel, after the Standards' adoption. In that document, and in various other commentaries, they suggest that students must make ideas *only* from within "the four corners of the text" and that prior knowledge should not be brought into discussions of text. The latter point, Timothy Shanahan noted, was removed from a revised version of their *Criteria* due to pushback from the educational research community (2013). Though the lead writers argue this as the way to meet the Standards, as many educators have found, if you remove the student from the process of reading, the reading goes, too. As Kylene Beers tweeted, "The Publishers' Criteria of the CCSS has assumed authority, not assessed. Don't do what you know isn't right" (@KyleneBeers April 21, 2013).

Instead of seeing this as a debate between two opposing sides, we believe there is a way to achieve both goals—to teach students to read more analytically, while also valuing their lives and experience. In fact, in this book we argue that by learning to read more closely, our lives and experience grow richer as well.

As we researched close reading practices, we looked for a way to define the approach that takes from the best of what is available. Figure 1.1 shows a vision for close reading that we have come to find effective for developing students' habits.

What Is Close Reading?

▶ It is an interaction between the reader and a text (Douglas Fisher in the online video interview, "Close Reading and the Common Core State Standards," April 3, 2012).

▶ It is about making careful observations of a text and then interpretations of those observations (Patricia Kain for the Writing Center at Harvard University, 1998).

▶ It involves rereading; often rereading a short portion of a text that helps a reader to carry new ideas to the whole text (Kylene Beers and Robert Probst in *Notice and Note*, 2012).

Fig. 1.1 What Is Close Reading?

Given these definitions, we set out to design a vision for close reading instruction that matches both the academic demands of the approach with the engagement needs of our students. As Staff Developers with the Reading and Writing Project at Teachers College, Columbia University, we have been lucky to work within schools across the country and around the world, and we've seen how educators like you pour your love and attention into developing students who share the same passion for reading as you have. From these experiences, we've identified some central tenets that we have come to believe must be true for any instruction to be effective and that should apply equally to teaching close reading practices (see Figure 1.2).

Put directly, close reading is something we should teach students *to do*, rather than something we just *do to* them. Douglas Fisher and Nancy Frey suggest a similar caution, that "close reading doesn't mean that you simply distribute a complex reading and then exhort [students] to read it again and again until they understand it" (Fisher and Frey 2012, 8). We agree and believe that close reading takes clear, engaging, transferable, and responsive instruction. Close reading instruction must lead to students' own thoughtful reading.

Close reading instruction is most effective as a powerful piece of a large, robust, and responsive literacy curriculum. As Donalyn Miller describes in *The Book Whisperer*, "No matter how long students spend engaged in direct reading instruction, without time to apply what they learn in the context of real reading events, students will never build capacity as

Powerful Close Reading Instruction

- ▸ must raise engagement and joy, not diminish it
- ▸ must lead to student independence, not dependence on teacher's prompting
- ▸ must be one piece of your reading instruction, not the only part of your instruction
- ▸ must allow time for students to read for extended periods and across many pages of text, not interrupt time spent reading with activities
- ▸ must be repeated across time and involve lots of opportunities for practice, not be a one-time, off-the-checklist activity
- ▸ must be designed in response to the strengths and needs of your students, not planned solely to match a book or fit a scope and sequence.

Fig. 1.2 Powerful Close Reading Instruction

readers" (2009). It is beyond the scope of this book to describe all parts of effective literacy instruction. For that we suggest turning to resources such as *The Book Whisperer*, Ellin Keene's *Talk About Understanding* (2012—the book's Appendix A is invaluable), Penny Kittle's *Book Love* (2012), Nancie Atwell's *The Reading Zone* (2007), Lucy Calkins, Kathleen Tolan, and Mary Ehrenworth's *Units of Study for Teaching Reading* (2010), and Cris Tovani's *Do I Really Have to Teach Reading?* (2004).

The approaches in this book are designed with these definitions and tenets in mind and aim to keep students at the center of our instruction, even as we focus more closely on the texts they are reading. In doing so, we write this book as a love letter. It is a love letter to the power and joy of reading and to supporting students in doing so with depth of thought and passion.

What You Will Find in This Book

This book is written to help you plan instruction that supports the development of close reading practices. It is organized to help you make decisions to best support your students.

- ▪ **An emphasis on students talking and processing, so you can quickly see their needs and next steps:** You will see a focus on students talking, problem solving, and developing ideas together. While we demonstrate the strategies, we turn the main thinking back over to the students. These are active, challenging, student-driven lessons. These are not "one-right-answer" ways of thinking, but instead offer opportunities for students to think broadly and then refine their ideas through careful analysis of text. Students do most of the heavy lifting here, so you can have what researcher John Hattie refers to as "visible learning," an essential feedback loop in your classroom in which continual feedback from student work informs your next instructional steps (2008).

- **Lessons written for a variety of contexts: texts, media, and life:** While close reading is indeed academic and often focused on written texts, you will find that we carry these strategies beyond the page and organize them as tools for living more reflective lives. Powerful literacy strategies tend to be powerful life strategies as well, and we aim to draw those extensions clearly for students. When you look carefully at characters in books, you learn to listen more carefully to the characters in the TV shows you are watching and to the people in your life. When you study how an author's words are chosen for effect, you can pay attention to words used in advertisements and learn to more carefully choose your own words with others. Every chapter is organized across these contexts:

  - a lesson centering around familiar media, from popular music to television shows
  - a main lesson analyzing one text type, informational or literature
  - a variation on the main lesson for the other text type
  - suggestions for ways to study the close reading skill in life, from the words students' peers use to how they structure their personal time.

- **Chapters organized from fundamental close reading skills to more complex applications:** The chapters then repeat these lessons across a variety of close reading skills. The first three chapters we see as fundamental skills: reading closely for text evidence (Chapter 2), word choice (Chapter 3), and structure (Chapter 4). Then later chapters suggest ways to combine these skills to do more advanced study: looking for point of view and argument (Chapter 5) and reading closely across texts (Chapter 6). Chapter 7 suggests a vision for students using these skills interchangeably, as well as ways you can organize your instruction to meet the needs of your students.

- **Extensions to support differentiation:** Each chapter ends with a section of additional lessons, organized as supports for students who need additional practice and instruction and extensions for students who are ready to move ahead.

- **Samples of grade-level lessons, charts, and student work from classrooms around the world:** While we find that these skills can be taught across years of schooling, we indicate specific grade levels for some lessons simply to provide context for our text choices and the language used. Each chapter includes sample charts to support students' skill development, as well as examples of students' work that came from the lessons and application to their own independent reading.

- **Book and media suggestions for lessons:** Throughout the chapters, we offer suggestions for best-loved texts and media, all culled from classrooms around the world. We have also placed QR codes throughout the book to help you connect directly to some of this media. There are many QR scanner apps available, most for free, for use with your smartphone or tablet.

- **Connections to the Common Core State Standards:** It is important to plan with goals in mind. One set of goals is your state's standards. As many states have adopted the CCSS, we provide descriptions of the Standards that connect to the central work of each chapter.

Teaching Within a Close Reading Ritual to Build Independence

We present a central structure that ties all of these lessons and chapters together. Much like a few key behaviors make up baseball (swing, hit, run) or cooking (chop, heat, stir), we have seen that by giving students a structure—or a ritual—to follow, they quickly become more independent. Structure can lead to habits, and habits can lead to independence. Our ritual for teaching students to read closely developed into three steps, steps that are connected and that help students navigate this complex skill set in more approachable ways:

1. First, read through **lenses**: Decide what you will be paying attention to while reading and collect those details.

2. Next, use lenses to find **patterns**: Look across all of the details you have collected and find patterns. As Dorothy Barnhouse and Vicki Vinton discuss in *What Readers Really Do* (2012), details alone do not mean much until you begin to see relationships across them.

3. Finally, use the patterns to **develop a new understanding of the text**: Consider these patterns in light of what you have already learned from the text. Put these together to develop a new understanding of the text or a deeper, evidence-based interpretation.

This ritual, then, can be the container for a wide range of teaching. Just as a baseball player learns variations and techniques to "hit" (bunt, line drive, grounder) and a chef can more artfully craft a meal as she develops ways to "heat" (steam, *sauté*, *sous vide*), throughout this book your readers will learn many ways to read with a lens, to find patterns, and to develop powerful understandings.

Falling in Love with Close Reading

We believe that, as human beings, we already know how to read something closely. Just think back to those loves at the beginning of this chapter; the details you study closely from that sweater you love or from that person you fell in love with. The patterns you find in how your child acts or how authors you admire write. Think about the ideas you develop about each of these things, and more so the ideas you develop about how they fit into your life.

You may not always realize you are doing these things, but that is just the point—we already know how to study what we love closely, it is a process, a method, of falling in love. The work, then, is to transfer this human ability to the texts we are reading, the texts that surround us, and to some of the areas of our life that may have gone unnoticed. That is the work of this book. It is our hope that you will fall in love with the potential of close reading as much as we have, and that your students will follow your lead.

So, let's begin. Grab your notebook, a pen, some best-loved books, maybe some colleagues, and let's go into your classroom together.

The Essence of Understanding
A Study of Text Evidence

We all yearn to be understood. We want a smile of recognition, a nod of heads in agreement, the feeling of community and connection that being truly understood brings. We choose what we say carefully in hopes of drawing other people to us, to have them understand just what we are trying to say, to feel connected. According to the field of cognitive relationship counseling, one of the most essential building blocks of a successful relationship is clear communication (Epstein and Baucom 2002). During a tough conversation, we can say to our partner, "I think I hear you saying," and repeat back that they felt you weren't listening when you glanced at the TV during dinner, then, through this retelling, realize that they *really* just wanted to feel more loved. We can observe our children carefully and look into their eyes and say, "Can I tell you what a great person you are?" and follow up with concrete examples of the way they give amazing hugs and how kindly they treat their friends. This is the stuff of our most important relationships: aiming to understand and be understood.

Texts strive to be understood in much the same way. Authors thoughtfully select details, hoping that we, the readers, are listening. When we take the time to do so, as carefully as we listen to the people we love, we see the complexity of ideas that reach beyond the page and impact our lives. In *The Art of Slow Reading* (2012), Thomas Newkirk describes this relationship between reader and text as an intimate one: "We commit ourselves to follow a train of thought, to mentally construct characters, to follow the unfolding of an idea, to hear a text, to attend to language, to question, to visualize scenes." When we become careful listeners of texts in this way, we smile in recognition, we nod our heads, and we create connections. This is the love that can come only from closely paying attention.

Take Marius. When reading *To Kill a Mockingbird* (1960), Marius aimed to understand as he paused and carefully considered Harper Lee's words. In Figure 2.1 he zooms in on the descriptions of Boo Radley's house, looking at the evidence closely to see what the author is trying to say.

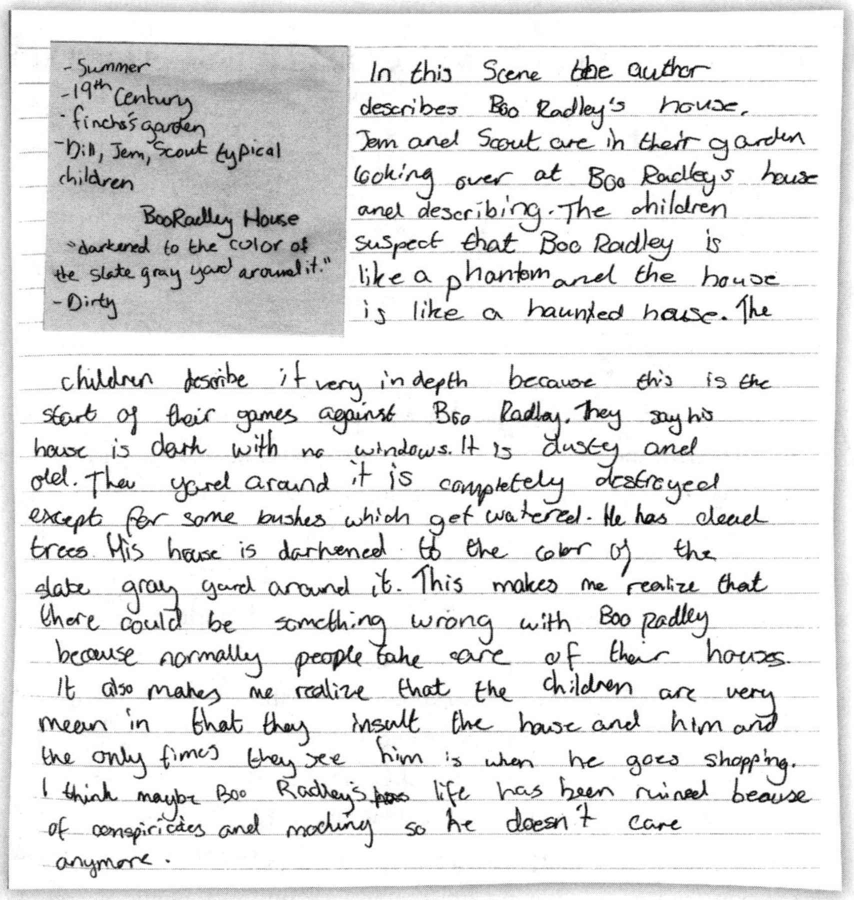

- Summer
- 19th Century
- finch's garden
- Dill, Jem, Scout typical children

BooRadley House
"darkened to the color of the slate gray yard around it."
- Dirty

In this Scene the author describes Boo Radley's house. Jem and Scout are in their garden looking over at Boo Radley's house and describing. The children suspect that Boo Radley is like a phantom and the house is like a haunted house. The children describe it very in depth because this is the start of their games against Boo Radley. They say his house is dark with no windows. It is dusty and old. Ther yard around it is completely destroyed except for some bushes which get watered. He has dead trees. His house is darkened to the color of the slate gray yard around it. This makes me realize that there could be something wrong with Boo Radley because normally people take care of their houses. It also makes me realize that the children are very mean in that they insult the house and him and the only times they see him is when he goes shopping. I think maybe Boo Radley's ~~pos~~ life has been ruined beause of conspiricies and mocking so he doesn't care anymore.

Fig. 2.1 Marius' Response to *To Kill a Mockingbird*

You can see the care with which Marius gathered descriptions of the house, and you can almost hear the moment of his realization—his empathy for Boo—as he comes to believe that the children are "very mean" and that Boo Radley's life "has been ruined because of conspiracies and mocking so he doesn't care anymore." Teaching our students to read for "caring understanding" can be teaching them to listen with caring understanding, and can lead them to *live* with this same caring understanding.

The Tools of the Trade: Getting Ready to Close Read for Text Evidence

Teaching students to read in this careful way involves helping them to acquire the vocabulary for talking about text. The more specific your language, the more you focus your attention and your thinking. If you tell a child how great she is, you can give vague praise: "Kid, you are *great*." But the more specifically you learn to describe a child's greatness, the more explicitly you will compliment her—for the generous things she does, for her sense of humor, for her intellect and creativity. Thinking "things she does," "things she says," "qualities she has" not only helps you to be more specific, it literally guides you to search out her qualities.

In narrative texts, for example, it helps to teach students some terminology for the kinds of evidence they are collecting and the types of ideas they aim to create. At the Reading and Writing Project, when we aim to support students in developing more specific thinking, we often find that the *more* words they use, the more precise their thinking becomes. There is a difference between saying, "I'm going to gather details" and "I'm going to pay attention to descriptions of the setting." Just as saying, "I'm going to have an idea" differs from, "I'm going to consider the type of relationship these characters have." We have collected some common ways to describe text evidence and ideas in narratives (see Figure 2.2), and later in the chapter, we include a similar chart for informational texts (see Figure 2.7 on p. 26).

Teaching students to read in this way also involves helping them transfer skills to their independent practice in more powerful ways. We often used to say to students, "Take your idea about the book, say '*because the text says*,' and then find a detail from the text to support your thinking." But what we mostly found was that students' initial ideas were overly simple, or too far removed from the text. As we studied this more closely, it turned out that the issue was not whether they could *cite*, the challenge was how they constructed their ideas in the first place. What we came to find is that helping students to develop clearer ideas often involves flipping the steps around:

1. *Now, students tend to*: have an idea, then go find evidence.

2. *Instead, we can teach*: gather evidence, then develop an idea.

This was just what Marius did when he *first* looked at the descriptions of Boo Radley's house, *then* developed ideas from those details. His ideas were more thoughtful and reflective of what he read because he began with the details.

This brings us back to the close reading ritual that we introduced in Chapter 1: three repeatable steps that students can learn to move through to develop new understandings of a text. Many teachers post this chart, or a variation of it, as a reference for students throughout this study. Here we include descriptions for narrative texts (see Figure 2.2).

	READING CLOSELY FOR **TEXT EVIDENCE**
1. Read through lenses.	Choose specific details to gather as data: • What characters/people: say/think/do • Relationships • Setting descriptions • Time period *(See Appendix for others.)*
2. Use lenses to **find patterns.**	• Which details fit together? • How do they fit together?

3. Use the patterns to **develop a new understanding of the text.**	Look at patterns to think about:
	• Character's/people's:
	  ◦ Feelings
	  ◦ Traits
	  ◦ Relationships
	• Whole text:
	  ◦ Themes
	  ◦ Lessons
	(See Appendix for others.)

Fig. 2.2 Close Reading Ritual: Text Evidence in Narrative Texts

Later, we revise the chart for nonfiction texts (see Figure 2.7 on p. 26). Other ideas are offered in the Appendix (see p. 126).

Closely Reading Media: Engage Students Through Popular Songs and Text Evidence

We believe that a powerful way to begin a study of text evidence is to start first with texts that surround us every day. In this case, students learn to see that what they once thought was true about a popular song can suddenly change after looking closely at its lyrics.

For this lesson:

> ▸ *Have an audio clip ready of a current popular song, as well as a printout of its lyrics, both of which are easy to find online.*
>
> ▸ *Optionally, invite students to print out and bring in song lyrics—with guidelines set by you—to some of their current favorite songs or hits their classmates are singing to. These extra sets of lyrics can provide independent practice after the lesson.*
>
> ▸ *Have the chart in Figure 2.2 on p. 12 or Figure 2.7 on p. 26 ready to refer to.*

In *The Art of Teaching Reading* (2001), Lucy Calkins describes how it is essential that we make our instructional goals clear to our students so that they can transfer our teaching to their practice. In this case, let your students know that you will help them see how close reading can lead them to have new ideas about something familiar in their lives. You could begin this lesson by saying:

> "Often, we have ideas about popular songs, not just from the songs themselves but because of what we are experiencing in our lives at the time. After a fight with someone you care about, every song sounds sad. And sometimes that is just what you need! But today I want to show you how listening and looking carefully at a song's lyrics can lead us to see things we may have missed before."

Your aim here is to help students have initial ideas while listening to a song, then to help them see how the process of looking more carefully at the song's lyrics can lead them to revise those ideas. Begin by playing a portion of the song, then, after listening, ask your students to talk with one another: "Can you describe to someone sitting next to you what the ideas in this song are, or what messages the song is trying to convey?" As you listen to their conversations, jot some of their comments down. With several classes, we have used "Boyfriend" by Justin Bieber (*Believe* 2012) because students generally either love or loathe him, and we want to capitalize on these strong emotions. When one group of fifth graders listened to the song, they first had ideas like "He wants to be her boyfriend" and "He thinks he would be a good boyfriend."

These QR codes are present throughout the book to connect you to media. See page 7 for more information.

Next, have students look at the printed lyrics of the song. Briefly demonstrate how you can now read, looking for details you may have missed the first time, in order to develop new ideas. Most students tend to spot new or surprising ideas in lyrics right away, however if your students need a nudge you could suggest particular kinds of details to look for, such as what the narrator of the song describes as his "thoughts" or "actions." For other suggestions, you could refer to the earlier chart for types of evidence you might read for, as well as some possible ideas to have about them (see Figure 2.2 on p. 12).

As students read the lyrics to "Boyfriend" closely for text evidence, they often begin to notice that the narrator mostly talks about how much money he has, the fancy things he could pay for on dates, and the trips he could take his love interest on.

Figure 2.3 shows fifth grader Zoe's notes, after looking carefully at these lyrics. At first, she collects the things she notices about the song. Then she shifts gears and begins thinking about what this text evidence tells us. She develops the idea (comma added for clarity), "He wants to be what the girl wants, not himself."

After your students' realization that reading song lyrics carefully can sometimes reveal once-hidden ideas, you might point out that popular songs, just like books—and even just

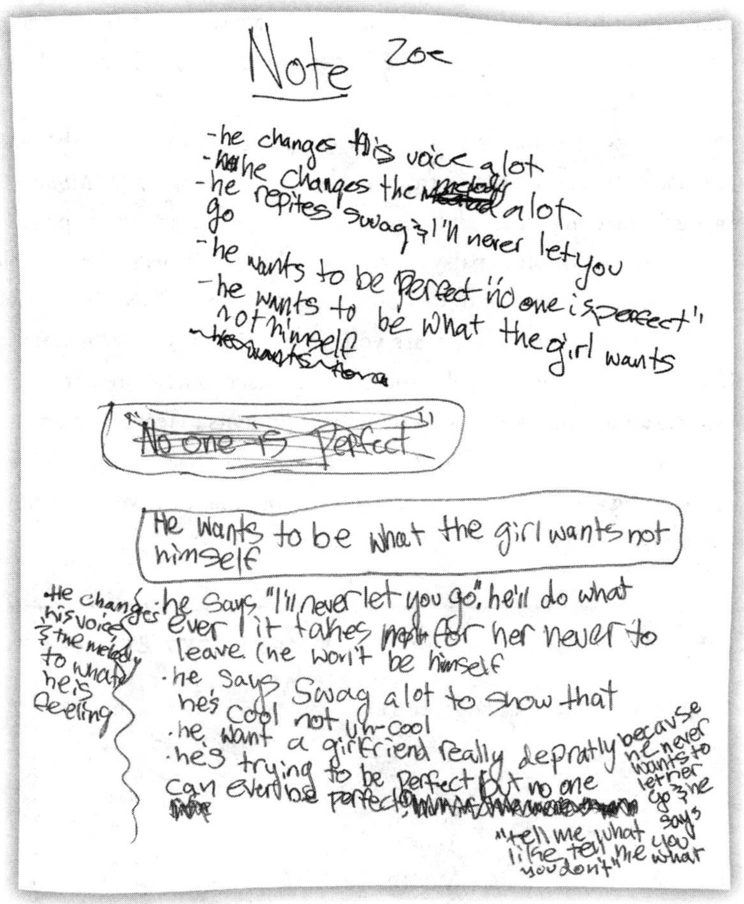

Fig. 2.3 Zoe's Response to the Lyrics of "Boyfriend"

like people—have messages they want to send out into the world. The more carefully we pay attention, the closer we read, the more that can be revealed.

More Than Just "Because": Closely Reading Narrative Texts to Analyze Evidence and Meaning

A close reading ritual like this can be used for a variety of purposes. Which purpose, or instructional goal, you choose to focus on will depend on a variety of factors, including the unit of study you are in and your assessment of your students. For this lesson, we chose to use our close reading ritual to help students to think more deeply about characters, because this felt specific enough as a guiding purpose for rereading while still leaving lots of room for students to develop their own thinking.

Working closely with students in Great Neck, Long Island, a suburb outside of New York City, we decided to use an excerpt from Sharon Draper's *Out of My Mind* (2012) for this lesson, a gorgeously written young-adult novel about Melody, a girl with a quick wit and photographic memory whose cerebral palsy makes communication nearly impossible for her.

Consider the texts you choose to demonstrate with carefully. Do they provide rich opportunities to do close reading work toward your instructional goal? Will your students find the text compelling so that they would want to come closer to it? Also take into account the challenge of the text; more accessible texts often help students to feel confident and allow you to see who is struggling with the *skills* of close reading, rather than with the *text*. Think of your work as spanning across the school year, and across that time you can move through a wide variety of texts and various levels of challenge.

	READING CLOSELY FOR TEXT EVIDENCE
1. Read through lenses.	Choose specific details to gather as data: • What characters/people: say/think/do • Relationships • Setting descriptions • Time period *(See Appendix for others.)*

In this lesson, we intend to guide students' thinking about characters through the ritual of close reading. We are treating this day as if it were the first close reading lesson in your class, and so we have chosen to spend a moment introducing the ritual first.

"Across your years of schooling, and even so far this year, you have thought a lot about the characters and people in the texts you are reading: the kind of people they represent, the things they do, how they interact, and so on. Today, I want to teach you a new sort of reading ritual that can build upon the great work you are already doing.

"Think about the rituals you see in your life and in the lives around you. There are big ones, like how weddings tend to go in your culture. There are smaller ones, like your own 'getting ready for school' ritual each morning. All rituals involve steps in a process and the feelings you bring to them. A graduation ritual typically involves a speech, students marching up to get their diplomas, and then families snapping pictures. It also involves having a joyful yet serious feeling; people dress up and treat it as a big life step. I want to take you through this new, close reading ritual and show you how it can be another way of reading that you can draw on.

"This ritual is for reading a text closely. It involves three steps: deciding what to carefully look for; finding what these things have in common, like a pattern; and then stepping back and seeing what new understanding this gives you about the text."

Be sure to make your instructional goal clear to your students. While this may be a lesson introducing the steps of reading closely for text evidence, show them how it can help them develop new ideas, like understanding their characters in deeper ways. Just as the writing process is a container for a wide variety of teaching, so the ritual of close reading is a tool for a wide variety of thinking.

"One reason to read a text closely is to help us think more powerfully about our characters, purposefully gathering details about them and then reflecting on what the evidence reveals. Close reading can help our thinking become precise, sophisticated, and interesting. Today we are going to focus specifically on what close reading for text evidence might reveal about the *characters* in our books.

"So to start, let's begin with the thinking we are doing now. We just read a bit from Chapter 3. Could you stop for a moment and write down some of your thinking about the characters in this section?"

As students jot down notes, look over their shoulders and choose one or two examples to share with the class. Try to look for general patterns across your class, such as noting that everyone is writing very brief ideas. Also know that at the end, you will revise the idea—so don't pick a very complex example, or you may be left with little to revise.

"I'd like to put two ideas on the board that I saw some of you writing: 'Melody's dad likes to sing' and 'Melody's dad is really nice to her.' These are solid ideas you are having about a character, a great place to start some close reading work.

"We can get better at thinking about a character if we choose specifically what to look for, what we call **a lens**, meaning we can choose what *kind* of evidence we might gather as we read. A lot of your ideas from this scene were about Melody's father, so let's pay attention to him and choose from our chart a kind of evidence or detail to read for (see Figure 2.2 on p. 12). How about what he *does* in this scene? This can be our **lens**—this will help us decide what evidence to pull out of the story. As we read, I am going to start a quick list of details that show '*Things Melody's father does.*' Can you open your notebooks and do the same? Let's reread this section":

> *Dad never spoke baby talk to me like my mother did. He always spoke to me as if he were talking to a grown-up, using real words and assuming I would understand him. He was right.*
>
> *'Your life is not going to be easy, little Melody,' he'd say quietly. 'If I could switch places with you, I'd do it in a heartbeat. You know that, don't you?'*
>
> *I just blinked, but I got what he meant. Sometimes his face would be wet with tears. He'd take me outside at night and whisper in my ear about the stars and moon and the night wind.*
>
> *'The stars up there are putting on a show just for you, kid,' he'd say. 'Look at that amazing display of sparkle! And feel that wind? It's trying to tickle your toes.'*
>
> *And during the day he would sometimes take off all the blankets that my mother insisted I be wrapped in and let me feel the warmth of the sun on my face and legs. (p. 11)*

"The **lens** of '*Things Melody's father does*' helped me to pay attention to particular details. Here is my list, you probably have something similar:

- *He doesn't speak baby talk to Melody like her mom does.*
- *He talks to Melody like a grown-up.*
- *He cries and wants to trade places with Melody.*
- *He whispers to her about the stars.*
- *He takes off the blankets Melody's mom says she needs to have on.*

"Okay, let's read a little bit more and collect a few more details using the same lens of '*Things Melody's father does.*'"

Read on a bit further, allowing students to collect more information. Students may collect evidence such as:

- *He put a bird feeder on the porch.*
- *He tells Melody the names of birds.*

- *He laughs.*
- *He sings to her.*

"So, I could have just read this part quickly and thought, 'Yeah, yeah, she and her dad did stuff together.' Instead, I have this list of details in my mind and on paper. Next, I want to show you how we can analyze these details by looking for patterns."

As we mentioned in Chapter 1, you could decide to make this the end of your day's lesson and continue with the next step when you feel your class is ready. If that is the case, then invite students to return to their own independent reading and practice the skill of choosing a lens and collecting text evidence with that lens. Direct students to your chart (see Figure 2.2 on p. 12), and invite them to search for what a character does—just as you have—or to try reading for other types of details.

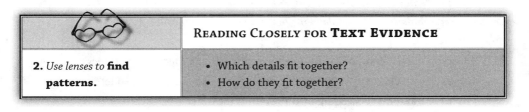

	READING CLOSELY FOR **TEXT EVIDENCE**
2. *Use lenses to* **find patterns.**	• Which details fit together? • How do they fit together?

Next, we want to support students in looking back across these details and seeing how some fit together and seeing overarching categories. In What Readers Really Do, *Dorothy Barnhouse and Vicki Vinton describe patterns as something writers deliberately create in their texts, "laying them down like breadcrumbs in a forest, for [her] readers to follow" (2012, p. 111). We love that breadcrumb image and agree with their take that finding patterns from gathered bits of text is where the real work of comprehension begins.*

"So, we have this list of details. If we are reading closely to analyze a character, it is helpful to look across the evidence we collected, to **look for patterns**, or groupings.

"Watch how I can do this with our list. I am going to reread it and see if there is some evidence that fits together. Like, maybe they are similar kinds of actions, or perhaps they have a similar effect or emotion. Or maybe the pattern we see is that there are details that show the character's relationship to others. For our purposes here, I think I'll draw a different shape around each pattern I see, or I could even color-code them and make a key on the side, like a map key. Then I can say, all the ideas in boxes have this in common, and all the ones in circles mean something else, and give each group a title.

"Watch me try. I'm going to reread our list and ask myself, 'Which details fit together?' and 'How do they fit together?' Well, I see some details that are the same because they are about the ways he speaks to Melody: he whispers, he cries, and so on. So for my key, maybe I will circle all of these details. Then I'll call it something, maybe: *'The ways Melody's dad speaks to her.'* **When looking for patterns**, aim to be specific—try to say both what you see and the quality of it. Instead, I could say, *'Melody's dad speaks to her in very caring ways.'*" (See Figure 2.4.)

"There are some details I didn't include. Could you turn to a partner and see if you could make up a group for those? Maybe we'll put a box around them . . ."

Have your students discuss in pairs. Predictably, there will be variations in how they describe a group of details or even determine which details go together. Don't worry if what students notice at this point are not big, earth-shattering analyses. Instead, the focus here is that the patterns students find should help the whole of the text evidence shine through.

"I heard a few different **patterns**. One was, *'Melody's dad teaches her things'* another was, *'Melody's dad does the opposite of her mom.'* I like them both, so let's put a box around one and maybe a squiggly line around the other.

"What we are doing is not just noticing details and stopping. Instead, we are noticing details and then doing a really important second step: we're seeing what **patterns are in those details**. Patterns help us see what is important."

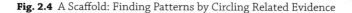

Fig. 2.4 A Scaffold: Finding Patterns by Circling Related Evidence

	READING CLOSELY FOR **TEXT EVIDENCE**

3. *Use the patterns to* **develop a new understanding of the text.**	Look at patterns to think about:
	• Character's/people's:
	  ◆ Feelings
	  ◆ Traits
	  ◆ Relationships
	• Whole text:
	  ◆ Themes
	  ◆ Lessons

It is essential that students develop ideas about the text, not just collect details. Some of your students will already have many new thoughts by this point. If that is the case, by all means, let them speak or write that thinking down the moment it comes. In this last step, we aim to help students to keep their ideas grounded in the text evidence they just analyzed.

"What I want you to remember most is that anything you do while reading is only worth it if it helps you to think more about your reading. What I mean is, it doesn't really matter if you pull out details about a character and figure out how those details fit together if you don't use all that work to **have new ideas**. Just look. Here are our first ideas from the very start of our lesson again: 'Melody's dad likes to sing' and 'Melody's dad is really nice to her.' These were OK starts, but don't you feel like you know so much more now?

"We have pulled out some text evidence and looked for patterns, like *Melody's dad speaks to her in many different, very caring ways*; *Melody's dad teaches her things*, and *Melody's dad does the opposite of her mom.* Now let's put all of this together to **have a new understanding** about the character. We can think about the kind of person Melody's dad is, or his traits. Or maybe his motivations, or why he does what he does. If you need some help revising your ideas, Figure 2.5 on page 22 shows a few examples of ways you could start on this chart.

"OK, I'm going to use a prompt to help get me started: **My thinking about Melody's father has changed because** I thought he just liked to sing, but now I am seeing that he might see singing as another way of teaching her. **I think this because the author wrote** about many different things Melody's father is teaching her.

"I can keep these same details in mind and try a different prompt: **The reason why Melody's dad** likes to sing **is because** it seems to make him feel closer to her. **I**

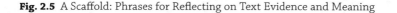

Phrases for Reflecting on Text Evidence and Meaning

▶ The reason why the character _____ is because _____.

▶ It seems like this character tends to _____.

▶ My thinking about this character has changed because _____.

▶ These characters are really different because _____.

▶ One issue I am noticing in this book is _____.

▶ I think the author is trying to teach me _____.

▶ I think this because the author wrote _____.

Fig. 2.5 A Scaffold: Phrases for Reflecting on Text Evidence and Meaning

think this because the author wrote a lot about how Melody's dad shares with her and teaches her many different things. Looking at our chart from earlier, and the kinds of ideas we can have about characters (see Figure 2.2 on p. 12), I can't help but notice that most of these ideas have to do with why Melody's dad does what he does—his motivations."

In this lesson, the purpose for close reading is for students to think more deeply about the characters in their books. Of course, we could have a different goal—to think about the setting, for example, and then collect setting descriptions and think about how the setting in this text feels. As we end the lesson, we want to check in on our original goal, while setting students up to practice this work on their own.

"When we look at our original ideas and put them next to the thinking we are having now, it seems like our close reading ritual is helping us to have more precise, sophisticated, and interesting ideas about the characters. Before you go off into your own books and try this yourselves, can you describe with a partner which parts of our ritual worked for you today, and which parts you want to get better at? Then get right into your books and begin trying out these steps on your own."

Watching students go back and revise their first ideas with collected and sorted text evidence is inspiring. They are often surprised by how simple their initial ideas about a character now appear and by how they now better understand what the text is trying to say because they took a bit of extra time to look closely.

Be sure, then, that students have time to practice these skills independently, in their own books. This more-support-to-less-support release of responsibility from teacher to student has long been an established model of effective teaching and learning (Vygotsky 1978; Pearson and Gallagher 1983; Mooney 1990). In the simplest terms: we only get good at the things that we do. As students work alone, assess what steps they will need more instruction for and time to practice with.

Cori, an eighth grader, practiced independently with a book she was reading on her own, *Jane Eyre* ([1847] 1991). While she was able to read this challenging book rather fluently—Cori is quite adept at handling challenging vocabulary and the speech patterns of British literature—she found that she was gathering major plot points but missing the more subtle comparisons and inferences. Here we see how this strong reader uses text evidence, finds patterns by color-coding, and then writes about some bigger ideas she formed. Notice that because Cori was working alone and not in conversation, she wrote a page about her thinking instead of just revising one idea (see Figure 2.6).

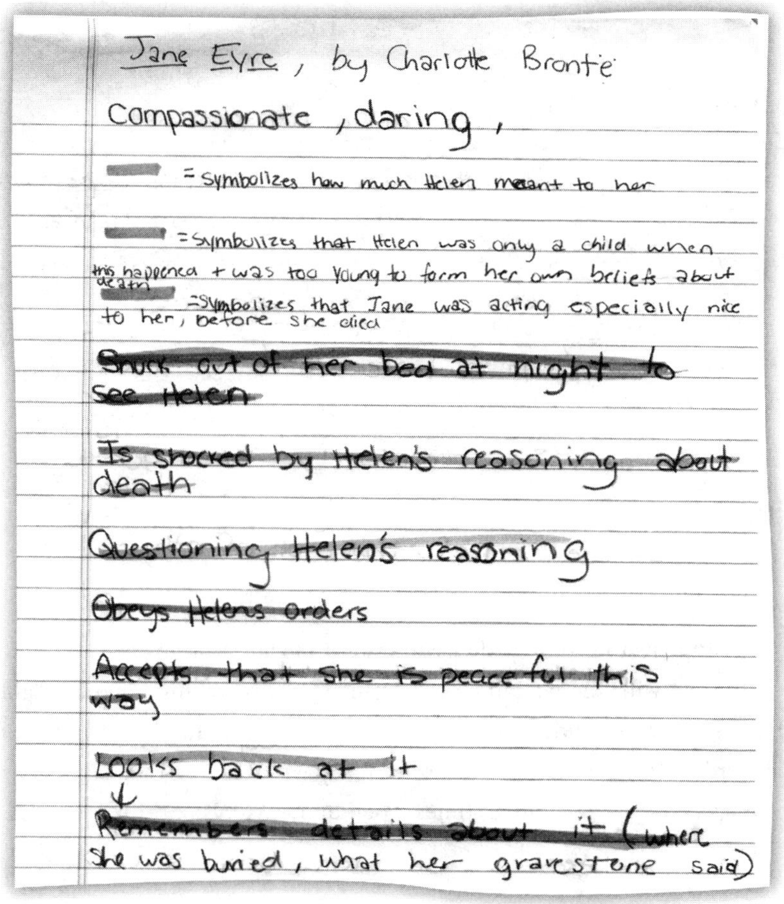
Jane Eyre, by Charlotte Bronte
Compassionate, daring,
= Symbolizes how much Helen meant to her
= Symbolizes that Helen was only a child when this happened + was too young to form her own beliefs about death
= Symbolizes that Jane was acting especially nice to her, before she died
Snuck out of her bed at night to see Helen
Is shocked by Helen's reasoning about death
Questioning Helen's reasoning
Obeys Helens orders
Accepts that she is peaceful this way
Looks back at it
↓
Remembers details about it (where she was buried, what her gravestone said)

Fig. 2.6a Cori's Response to *Jane Eyre* (continues)

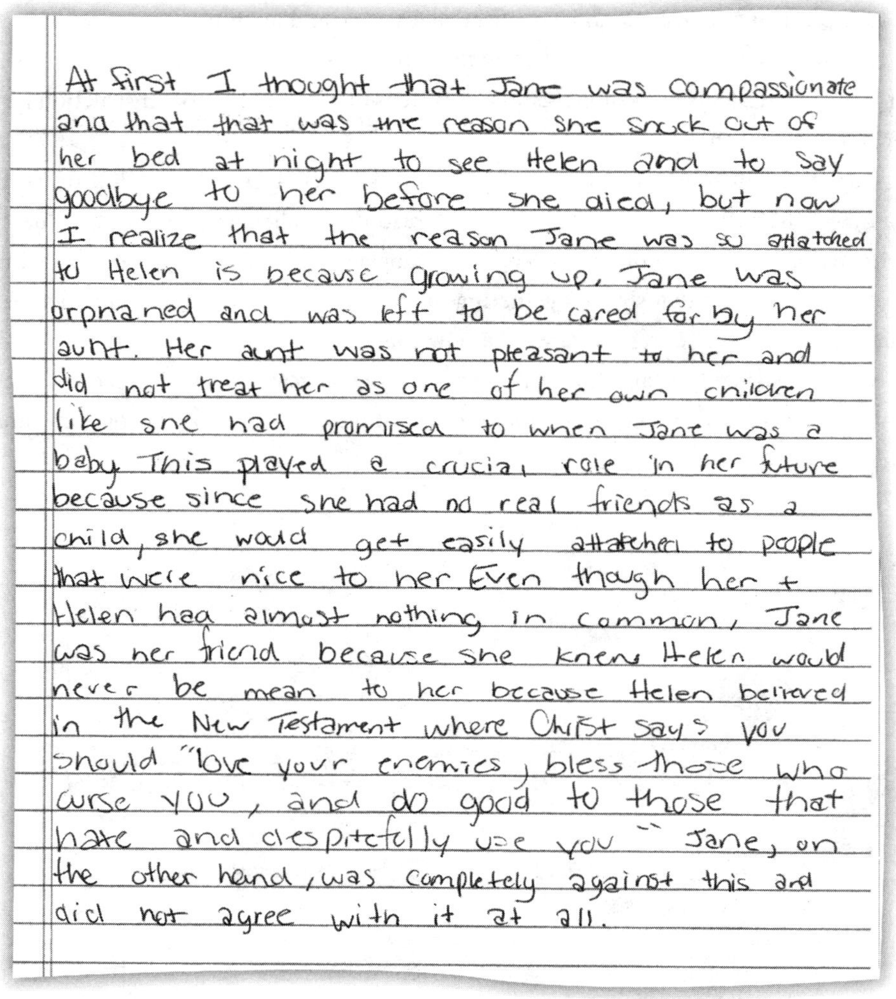

At first I thought that Jane was compassionate and that that was the reason she snuck out of her bed at night to see Helen and to say goodbye to her before she died, but now I realize that the reason Jane was so attached to Helen is because growing up, Jane was orphaned and was left to be cared for by her aunt. Her aunt was not pleasant to her and did not treat her as one of her own children like she had promised to when Jane was a baby. This played a crucial role in her future because since she had no real friends as a child, she would get easily attached to people that were nice to her. Even though her + Helen had almost nothing in common, Jane was her friend because she knew Helen would never be mean to her because Helen believed in the New Testament where Christ says you should "love your enemies, bless those who curse you, and do good to those that hate and despitefully use you." Jane, on the other hand, was completely against this and did not agree with it at all.

Fig. 2.6b Cori's Response to *Jane Eyre*

Teaching students to gather evidence in order to form ideas gives them the tools to interact more deeply with the texts they read. This is not searching for one "right" answer, instead this is supporting students in listening to the words of the author as carefully as you would the words of a close friend. It is an intimacy with reading that can yield surprising understandings about a book and, at times, open up new ways of thinking about people in the world.

The Facts We Choose to Tell: Modifying the Lesson to Analyze Text Evidence in Informational Texts

Whether or not we comprehend a text becomes more obvious when reading informational texts; let's face it, it is much harder to hide your uncertainty. I am sure we all remember faking our way through a class discussion of a novel we hadn't read, but nothing matches the fear of staring at a science quiz that makes no sense because you barely made it through the textbook. There are many valuable purposes for reading closely for text evidence in informational text—doing so to help you gain a stronger understanding of the text is one of them. You can also use a lenses/patterns/understandings ritual like we did in the previous lesson, only here we aim to teach students to make sense of any confusing parts of an informational text.

Here is a brief look at one article we have been using. It comes from *Science News for Kids*, an award-winning online science magazine. "Fooling the Mind's Eye" (Mascarelli 2013) describes the emerging field of "neuromagic," in which neuroscientists are studying how magic tricks fool our minds in order to unlock more of the brain's secrets. In the second section of the article, the language becomes particularly dense and full of important information that is in danger of being skipped. This means that when we stop to gather our rough, first-draft ideas, that idea is often "huh?" At that point in the lesson, we stop to jump into reading closely for text evidence to help clarify understanding:

> *Each human eye has a conduit to the brain called the optic nerve. It transmits all of the visual information that the eye takes in. The brain processes these data to fit with reality as we know it.*
>
> *An optic nerve consists of more than one million axons, or wirelike structures, bundled tightly together. They carry messages in the form of electrical impulses away from neurons, or brain cells. A few million axons may sound like a lot of capacity, [neuroscientist Stephen] Macknik admits. But compare that, he says, to an iPhone with an 8-megapixel camera. The camera has about four times the resolution—the capability to produce detailed images—of both of our eyes together. But the phone still takes poor pictures compared with how the world appears through human eyes. That's because the brain enriches our perception to make the world appear clearer, explains Macknik.*

When we teach this lesson, we first ask students to describe what they are confused about, to be specific about what they want to figure out. With this article, many students say they want to figure out "this *optic nerve* stuff." So we go back through those paragraphs to **read with the lens** of the text evidence that surrounds that idea or subtopic. We can refer to a chart similar to the one we used for our fiction lesson, but that now includes descriptions for informational texts. This can help us again to decide what kind of evidence to collect, as well as what kind of ideas we might strive to have (see Figure 2.7).

	READING CLOSELY FOR TEXT EVIDENCE
1. Read through lenses.	Choose specific details to gather as data: • Facts • Phrases • Descriptions • Photos or graphics *(See Appendix for others.)*
2. *Use lenses to* **find patterns.**	• Which details fit together? • How do they fit together?
3. *Use the patterns to* **develop a new understanding of the text.**	Look at patterns to think about: • Definitions of unknown terms or concepts • Central idea of an entire text • Author's bias or point of view *(See Appendix for others.)*

Fig. 2.7 Close Reading Ritual: Text Evidence in Informational Texts

Using the chart, we decide to list out the *facts* and *phrases* that feel confusing, such as:

♦ "transmits all of the visual information"

♦ "consists of more than one million axons"

♦ "they carry messages in the form of electrical impulses"

♦ "the brain enriches our perception"

Often, this is where students (and adults) stop when reading confusing informational text. We notice it is hard and then move on, hoping that the rest of the text will make it clear as we go. But by striving to **find the patterns** within these confusing facts and phrases, understanding can begin to emerge.

When using patterns to figure out unfamiliar informational texts, we once again look across collected details to see which fit together and what they have in common. Perhaps students will still want to color-code their information as they did in the previous lesson, this time looking for facts that seem to fit together. Students often see a pattern emerge. They notice that all of the facts and phrases they pulled out have to do with carrying information and what the brain does with that information. They can then step back and instead of saying "huh?" they can say, with some confidence, that all of these facts and phrases are about "how our brain gets and deals with information."

We can then return to the text to **develop a clearer understanding.** Using the chart shown in Figure 2.7, we can decide to find a *definition* for what optic nerves do. (In addition, you could create a chart of prompts similar to Figure 2.5 on p. 22 to help your students to become idea generators, if you observe that they are having trouble on their own.) We take what we knew originally, "something about an optic nerve," and put it together with the new patterns we are finding: that this section of the article is mostly about "how our brain processes what we see." So we think, *Does this help me* define *how optic nerves work? Yes! I can see that this text is teaching me that optic nerves carry information to the brain.*

In this lesson, we have focused on looking at confusing facts and phrases and coming up with some definitions and central ideas. These same steps could be used interchangeably with other types of evidence and other kinds of ideas.

Now, your first attempt at helping students make sense of confusing informational text may not go perfectly, but keep your focus on teaching students these steps and skills, not just on having them get things correct on the first try. What you will most likely find is that even if students are not developing a totally accurate idea, their work with lenses and patterns will lead them to a more closely aligned idea than their first reading did.

This commitment to focusing on text evidence to understand informational texts is critically important to our students as readers, not to mention a critical skill in life as well. Whether reading a long lease agreement before renting an apartment or aiming to understand course material for an unfamiliar subject, the ability to focus in on what is confusing and not give up—but instead do more with it—is empowering.

Next Steps: Extensions and Support for Close Reading of Text Evidence

As you teach students to gather text evidence, analyze it, and develop new understandings, plan to pay careful attention to what they produce when working independently. Your assessment of their independent work can help you decide on next steps.

You may find, for example, that your students' ideas from the text evidence in narratives feel vague. In the chart shown in Figure 2.8, there are a few strategies to make our thinking more sophisticated, with examples of an idea becoming more complex by using those strategies. Here we are imagining a student, who after analyzing evidence about Susan "Stargirl" Caraway from Jerry Spinelli's *Stargirl* (2000), comes to the simple idea that "she is brave."

Ways to revise our thinking	*Example of revising the idea "she is brave"*
Use the *exact word* you mean. Make sure that every word you use is the best one.	*She has a bold, unafraid personality.*
Use *qualifying language* to say more. Qualifying language includes answers to "when," "how," "for whom," "what kind," or "why."	*She has a bold, unafraid personality when she goes to school, because she seems not to care what people think.*
Look for *causes or effects*, problems or solutions that are being expressed in the evidence. Often, these are more sophisticated ideas.	She has a bold, unafraid personality when she goes to school, because she seems not to care what people think. *She does this to cover up the fact that she really wants people to like her.*

Fig. 2.8 Ways to Revise Our Thinking

This is one example of responding to a need you see in your students' work with close reading for text evidence. Next, we suggest a few other options for providing extra support and extensions.

Additional Lessons for Providing Extra Support

- **Use conversation to evaluate collected evidence:** If you find your students are collecting a lot of rambling or sporadic text evidence, teach them to be more selective with their details. One vehicle for this can be small-group inquiry. Heather Rocco, a Supervisor of English Language Arts, grades 6–12, in New Jersey, suggests that students return to a familiar passage and select one detail they believe is most important. Students share these details, and the group listens for similarities. Then, help students describe the characteristics of meaningful details. As you work together, refer back to your anchor chart (see Figure 2.2), making connections to what you have previously taught, such as saying, "Sometimes details that show things about characters' relationships are worth paying close attention to."

- **Rank evidence to see which idea it supports:** If you find that the connection between the text evidence students collect and the ideas they are having is weak, try having them rank the evidence they find. Teach students to sort their evidence by which detail best supports their thinking, which does not go with the idea, and which asks us to revise our ideas.

- **Know *when* to close read for text evidence:** If your students are great at using these skills with you while you are teaching but struggle to apply them with their own books, then teach them *when* to initiate their newfound abilities. You could begin a lesson by inviting students to brainstorm when it feels important to read closely for text evidence. In nonfiction, for instance, when the author seems to be making a major point or, as we mentioned earlier, when you find yourself confused by jargon. In fiction, you might stop to read closely during an emotional scene or when a new character is introduced.

Additional Lessons for Providing Advanced Work

- **Expand our lenses:** If students appear adept at using single lenses independently, then invite them to hold onto more lenses at any one time. Some helpful first steps: revisit a familiar passage, this time carrying more than one type of detail to look for. Some students may be able to do this in their head, others may want to write a T-chart of the different kinds of evidence they are collecting. As an alternative, teach students to look for text evidence for more than one character or subject at the same time.

- **Seek out contrasting patterns:** If students appear to find patterns quickly in collected text evidence, then teach them to purposefully seek out contrasting patterns. As Donna Santman points out in *Shades of Meaning*, complexity is "the ability to hold in your mind two seemingly contradictory ideas and try to reconcile them" (2005). While both ideas will not always be present, the act of searching can lead to more careful consideration of the text. Go back to a text you have used, and show students how you take a pattern you have already found and return to find evidence that contrasts it in some way. For example, how characters say one thing but do another or how an author describes a subject mostly one way but in a few instances points to another view to consider.

- **Use analytical lenses for text evidence:** If students are showing signs of mastering the lenses you have taught them, then teach them to develop some more analytical lenses for text evidence. Reading for evidence that reveals social issues, power, gender, and so on allows students to begin forming not just ideas, but interpretations of their texts. Katherine and Randy Bomer's *For a Better World: Reading and Writing for Social Action* (2001) provides thoughtful approaches and an invaluable list of lenses like these.

Closely Reading Life: Looking at Specific Details in Our Lives

As students learn to look carefully at the text evidence an author provides and to use that evidence to make more focused and grounded ideas about a text, you have an opportunity to support them in thinking carefully about their lives as well. One way to do this is to look closely at the details we, and the people around us, choose to include in our lives. Just as an author decides upon particular text evidence, we make decisions every day about the life evidence that defines us. Invite your students to look closely at the choices they, and others, make:

- **Study personal style details:** What items, brands, or styles do your friends choose to wear? What might that say about them? What about other peers from your school who you do not know as well? What patterns of choices do you see?

- **Study the events leading up to a disagreement:** When you or a friend are in a conflict, go back to the facts. What happened, exactly? What was said, exactly? Look for the patterns and think about what it is that upset each party. Strive for text-evidence style truth rather than embellishment.

- **Study details *we* choose for ourselves:** Look at your room, your music, your actions, and your words. What patterns do you see in the way you are in the world? What do they have in common? What effect do they have on you, your friends, and your family?

- **Run experiments on authoring new patterns:** Try picking some piece of evidence about yourself—perhaps the fact that you proudly do not exercise, or the type of music you listen to—and change it for a week. See what effect it has on you, whether or not people notice, and what their reaction is. We can always change our behaviors, and sometimes these behaviors have powerful ramifications in our lives.

By looking at the evidence in a text, we see the ideas and traits within the details. And by looking at the evidence in our lives—our actions, belongings, and appearance—we can see that these things have a great effect on us and on the world around us. This knowledge can lead us to see ourselves, and those around us, more carefully and lovingly.

Take Theresa and Stephanie. In a StoryCorps recording, Theresa Nguyen talks with her adult daughter Stephanie, and they recollect the challenges of growing up first-generation Vietnamese American (storycorps.org).

Specifically, mother and daughter talk about conflicting interpretations of "life evidence" between Vietnamese culture and American culture. When Stephanie was younger, she was embarrassed that her mom asked her to return a necklace a boy gave her, but from her mother's heritage this symbolized a debt one would carry to their grave. At twelve, sleeping over at a friend's house meant everything to Stephanie, but to her mother it meant the family was not kept together. Through comparing not just the details of their lives, but how they interpreted them differently, both women came to understand each other more and, ultimately, their feelings about one another. The interview ends with Stephanie worrying that she was a disappointment. Her mom responds, "No you are not! I am just one of those old Asian moms. We never say we love you! We expect you to see it through our actions . . . When I go away from this life, I want you to remember my love for you, that's all. I don't care for anything else."

The practice of paying attention to life's details and carefully arranging them into ideas is one that brings us to a deeper understanding of all we hold dear—the books we enjoy, the songs that soundtrack our days, and the relationships we value most.

3

A Way with Words
A Study of Word Choice

I t is an exciting time to be young. Our students are growing up surrounded by more text and media than at any other time in human history. By some estimates, in the span of one year, roughly one million books are published and over one trillion web pages of information are accessible ("Did You Know 4.0," YouTube video 2009). Never before has so much information been so readily available. Global events unfold in real time across social networks, and questions can be researched and answered in mere moments. Our students are growing up in a world where knowledge and experience is just waiting to be harnessed.

This means our role in students' development is changing in an exciting way. No longer are we simply helping students find information, we are now in the position of empowering them with the vital habits of carefully sifting through all the sources that vie for their attention. One way we can do this is to teach students to be alert and attentive to language, to weigh the ways in which media, texts, and people select their words to subtly form their messages. We can teach them to be the kinds of readers who notice that:

- in the run up to an election, income taxes are called either "social-minded revenues" or "out-of-control spending"
- high-fructose corn syrup is either "unnatural poison" or "just corn"
- a morning-show segment on summer clothing either "flatters your figure" or "hides your flaws."

Looking closely at word choice allows us to get to the heart of what people are saying and thinking; it helps us see their motivations more clearly and decide how we wish to understand them.

For instance, Soren, a sixth grader, was reading *Nightrise* (2007) by Anthony Horowitz and stopped to think carefully about the words the narrator was using. He noticed how a description of an event did not seem to match the facts of what was going on, and this led him to think more about how dangerous a character seems (see Figure 3.1).

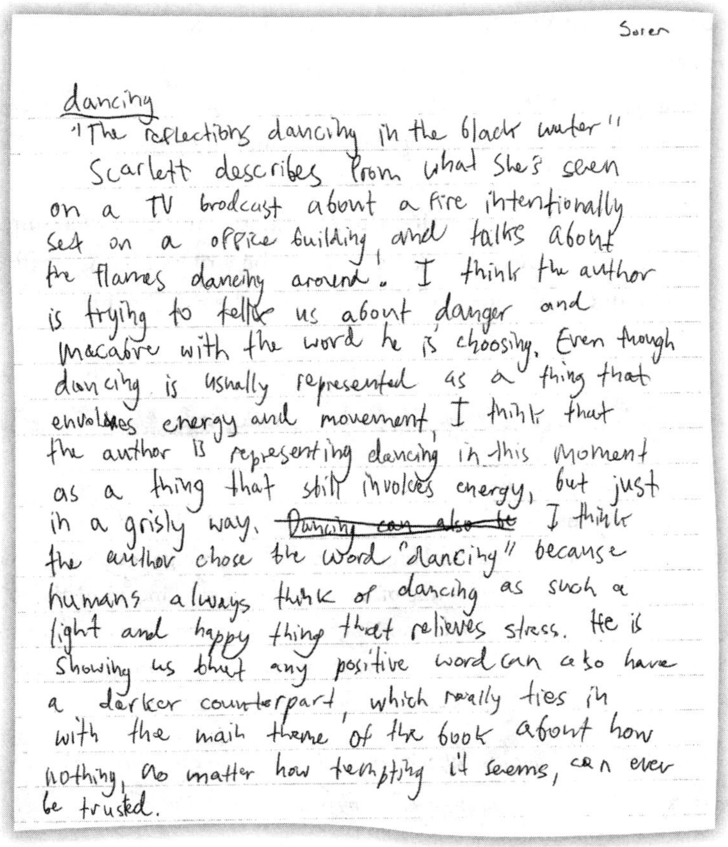
Soren

dancing

"The reflections dancing in the black water"

Scarlett describes from what she's seen on a TV brodcast about a fire intentionally set on a office building, and talks about the flames dancing around. I think the author is trying to tell us about danger and macabre with the word he is choosing. Even though dancing is usually represented as a thing that envolves energy and movement, I think that the author is representing dancing in this moment as a thing that still involves energy, but just in a grisly way. ~~Dancing can also be~~ I think the author chose the word "dancing" because humans always think of dancing as such a light and happy thing that relieves stress. He is showing us that any positive word can also have a darker counterpart, which really ties in with the main theme of the book about how nothing, no matter how tempting it seems, can ever be trusted.

Fig. 3.1 Soren's Response to *Nightrise*

From noticing the simple, seemingly positive description of a large, dangerous fire, he came to see this character as not being a very trustworthy narrator. In this, Soren sees that further meaning can be found in the words an author chooses.

The Tools of the Trade: Getting Ready to Close Read for Word Choice

Reading in this way is contemplative, similar to the way religious scholars, deep in their cloisters, seek out a profound understanding of life within the words of sacred texts. Or the way an agent pours over an encrypted document, full of intrigue, searching for a way to crack the code. Across the book, we refer to close reading as a ritual because we call on these feelings in students when they choose to read in this way. Like all rituals, the steps become second nature the more you experience them. To help students become independent with these skills, we aim to connect past learning (for instance, the steps we introduced in Chapter 2) with new learning (the new lens, or way of reading, we will develop here), and provide plenty of time for practice and feedback (National Research Council 2000).

Our students read words all day long, but oftentimes they (and perhaps we) use them mostly as tools for understanding. A close reading ritual for word choice shifts this, making words both something to gather meaning from and also something to admire the craft of and to interpret. In a sense, we ask students to make the writers of those texts come to life, to imagine actual authors and journalists pouring over their drafts thinking, "Should I use

---

❧ Standards and Close Reading for Word Choice

The Common Core State Standards expect that, by the end of the grade, students can "interpret words and phrases as they are used in a text" (R.4). There is a notable shift from elementary school to middle and high school. In the younger grades, students are expected to "determine the meaning of words and phrases," including that of some figurative language (RL.5.4). In middle and high school, students are expected to become increasingly more analytical, able to "analyze the impact of . . . word choice" an author makes (RL.6.4). You know students are developing these skills when:

▶ *they start describing not just what a text is about, but how it is written*

▶ *they refer to the author more often, either by name or generally.*

READING CLOSELY FOR **WORD CHOICE**	

1. Read through lenses.	Choose specific words to gather:
	• Words that evoke:
	   ◆ Strong emotions
	   ◆ Strong images
	   ◆ A clear idea
	(See Appendix for more examples.)

2. *Use lenses to* **find patterns.**	• Which words fit together? • How do they fit together?
3. *Use the patterns to* **develop a new understanding of the text.**	Think about an author's: • Tone • Purpose • Relationship to the subject • Central idea *(See Appendix for more examples.)*

Fig. 3.2 Close Reading Ritual: Word Choice in Narrative and Informational Texts

this phrase or this other one?" and making those choices with a purpose. Katie Wood Ray, in *Wondrous Words* (1999), calls reading in this way as having a "craft person's vision," which she describes as similar to how a gardener looks carefully at yards when driving down the street or how a dressmaker watches the fashion choices of people walking by; that readers look at texts and imagine how they were made.

Here is how we see a study of word choice translated into the same close reading ritual that was introduced in the previous chapter. Note that while the steps have remained the same, we have revised the contents of the chart to match this new study (see Figure 3.2).

Closely Reading Media: Engage Students Through Television Ads and Word Choice

One way to invite students to live looking for word choice is to study television advertising, those thirty-second spots that flood our screens, day after day. We can help students see that in all media, as well as in daily life, *everyone* chooses their words for a purpose.

You could begin by saying:

"Advertisements spin past us all day long, on TV, in sidebars on the Internet, and even popping up in apps on phones. Here is the thing, those ads are not just trying to sell us things; they are often also trying to sell us ideas about ourselves, trying to manipulate our self-image to motivate us to feel that we absolutely, positively, must have what they are selling. We're going to study how authors and advertisers choose their words carefully and how those words can subconsciously affect our thinking if we're not careful to notice them."

Guide your students to look carefully at the choices the commercial designers made, both in the words that are spoken (see Figure 3.2 on p. 35) and in the production choices (images, colors, actors, setting, fonts, and so on). In our lessons, we have been showing a Nerf gun toy commercial and a Lalaloopsy doll commercial and asking students: "Can you listen carefully to the words used in both commercials and the images you see and jot those down? Be ready to talk about what you are noticing."

Crystal Smith, on her blog *The Achilles Effect,* has done a similar experiment, studying a collection of "boy" toy commercials and "girl" toy commercials and pulling out the most commonly used words. She created word clouds to show how advertisers market their products when focusing on particular genders (see Figures 3.3 and 3.4).

Studying word choice opens up many possibilities for close reading. In Maureen Cassarino's eighth-grade class, for example, students reflected on the impact and effectiveness of word choice in advertisements during the Super Bowl, knowing that these thirty-second spots are prized moments for advertisers. Here, Jackie was using her tablet computer to reflect on a 2013 Super Bowl truck commercial that used Paul Harvey's speech "So God Made a Farmer" (1978) as a voice-over. Jackie thought about the ad's choice of words, what they would mean to a listener, and what effect they have in a car commercial (see Figure 3.5).

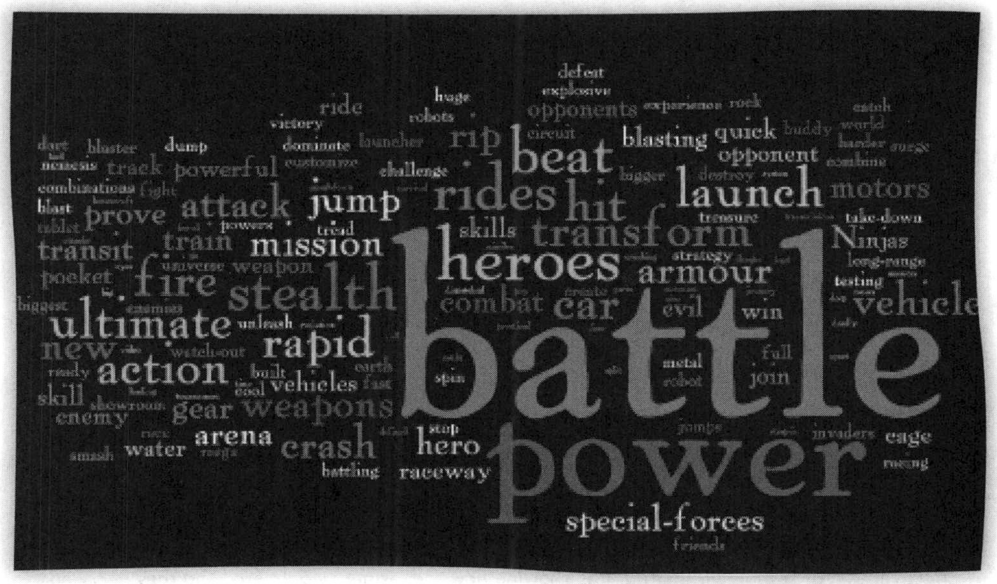

Fig. 3.3 Words Most Used for Toys Marketed to Boys

Fig. 3.4 Words Most Used for Toys Marketed to Girls

Words	Impact	Idea
Strong	Shows that the farmer is working hard. Shows that they're physically strong.	Not everybody has to be a farmer. There are many kinds of strengths.
Hard work	The hard work pays off Inspiring words of speech	The hard work represents the car. I think this because it's like a big, powerful car, which represents the hardworking farmer = hardworking car.
"God made a farmer"	Blessed to be a farmer. God blessed them with their job. Impact: powerful words of speech, repeated.	It's so important, that God made it.

Effectiveness for strong: I think that it is showing how the farmers work hard. And they're trying to show that the car works hard. It's big. "It can carry a workload."

Effectiveness for "God made a farmer": Powerful words of speech. It really helped the audience because of the repetition. At the end of the commercial I remembered the words. They really stuck in my head and made me think about the common farmer.

Fig. 3.5 Jackie's Response to Word Choice in an Advertisement

Raising students' awareness of how words are used in advertising can help them tune their close reading ears. It can help them see the power of language and how words can shape the way we think about events, products, and even ourselves.

"Macroscopic" vs. "Really Big": Closely Reading Informational Texts to Analyze Word Choice and Tone

As we use the steps of this close reading ritual in a new way, we want to be sure students understand that we are not just close reading for close reading's sake, instead we are using this process as a tool for thinking about the texts we are reading. Our purpose in this lesson is to teach students to closely read an informational text for word choice in order to examine the author's tone, and, ultimately, how the author's tone helps to develop the central ideas of a text. You, of course, will choose the instructional goal that best fits your students and your curriculum.

We have enjoyed teaching this lesson in many classrooms. On this particular day we were with Molly Magan's sixth graders in Queens, NY, a vibrant class made up of students with and without IEPs, some English Language Learners, and all from one of the most diverse neighborhoods in the United States, Jackson Heights. Coming during a particularly rough flu season in New York City, we decided it was fitting to use the article "Hand Washing" (Nemours Foundation 2011) from teenshealth.org.

For this lesson, we chose a text that felt topical and timely and that also had just enough "yuck" factor to really engage the students. Another way to select texts is to choose something that fits with a class topic or the content your class is learning in social studies, science, or related arts. Whatever you choose, keep in mind the importance of student engagement, and consider choosing texts based on either interest, relevance, or the context of their academics.

	READING CLOSELY FOR **WORD CHOICE**
1. Read through lenses.	Choose specific words to gather: • Words that evoke: 　◦ Strong emotions 　◦ Strong images 　◦ A clear idea *(See Appendix for more examples.)*

To begin, have students jot down their rough, first-draft ideas about what the informational text is teaching them. Similar to the work we did in Chapter 2, this will help us to see the power of studying word choice when we reflect on these ideas at the end of the lesson.

> "When we read informational texts, we read to figure out what an article is teaching us. I am going to read the first three paragraphs of this article. Can you listen and be ready to write down what you think this part is mostly about?"

As students record their main ideas, jot one or two on the board that you can return to and revise later on in the lesson. Look for an example or two of a main idea from this part of the text. If your students have trouble with this skill, you may need to support them in seeing larger ideas from text evidence. Chapter 2 can support that type of study, as well as professional texts such as Stephanie Harvey and Anne Goudvis' Strategies That Work *(2000) and Lucy Calkins and Kathleen Tolan's* Navigating Nonfiction *(2010).*

"A lot of you are saying similar things, that this article is mostly about, 'You should wash your hands' or 'Wash your hands so you don't get germs.'" Those are strong ideas and good starts. But we know now that our first thoughts are sometimes not the best ones we can have, and that our close reading ritual can help us to make our thinking stronger and more sophisticated. Today, we are going to see how close reading for the words an author chooses helps us to think about more than just what the text is teaching us—it can help us to analyze the tone or mood of the piece.

"Now, I want to show you something. Remember when we were looking at those advertisements? You had so much to say after paying close attention to the words the advertisers were using. You can use that same careful listening and apply it to when you are reading as well. When we decide to **read with the lens** of word choice, we look carefully at the *kinds of words and phrases* an author has chosen to use.

"Let's reread and make note—either on paper or just in your mind—of words or phrases that stand out to you. Using our chart of the kinds of words we can look for (see Figure 3.2 on p. 35), let's listen for words or phrases that give you a strong emotion or a clear image in your mind. I am going to reread and share with you a few that I am noticing:

> *'Wash your hands!' How many times have you heard that from your parents? You might think they're just nagging you, but actually the most important thing you can do to keep from getting sick is to wash your hands.*

"On my list, I already have a few words or phrases that stand out to me: 'nagging you,' because I can really picture my parents doing that. The author doesn't just say, 'your parents tell you,' the text says 'nagging.' Also 'getting sick,' I can almost feel that feeling. As I notice these words, I am *feeling* them too—like they mean more than just their definition—it's also about the emotion the words carry, their connotation.

"I am going to reread the next two paragraphs. Could you keep using this **lens of word choice** and jot down words and phrases that feel like choices to you, specifically ones that give you a strong image or strong emotion?"

We sometimes find that you need to give students a bit of a running start, so you may want to read more slowly at first, even pausing briefly after a phrase to highlight a particular word. This is a different kind of reading and listening than many students are used to, and giving them a little time to process at first can help.

"I saw some of your lists, and they look similar to words I was jotting down for myself as well:

- *disease*
- *frequently*
- *germs*
- *infect*
- *risk*
- *common*
- *virus*
- *sick*
- *spread germs*

"Nice work! When you **read with the lens** of word choice, you start to realize how many choices this author has made."

	READING CLOSELY FOR **WORD CHOICE**
2. *Use lenses to* **find patterns.**	• Which words fit together? • How do they fit together?

One potential pitfall for these kinds of lessons is that students will just return to their own books and hunt-and-peck for words, any words, and make overgeneralizations about them. This next step helps to reign that in as students start looking for not just single instances of word choice, but for patterns of choices starting to pop up across a text.

"Now, we don't just want to jump around, only talking about random words we notice in the text. As we zoom in, we should start looking for **patterns**, to see if the words the author chose fit together in some way. Then, when I try to explain the patterns I see, I can use some prompts that might help me to describe those patterns.

"Our first step is to look back at the word list we made and look for *groups*. Are there ways these words fit together? This is an important point—do not look for the meaning of the words. If I were talking about meaning, I might say about our list, 'all of these words have to do with being sick,' which is kind of obvious. Instead, I want you to study these words and start by **looking for patterns** of tone, or *feelings* the words give you. Are these words that are silly, scary, or sad? Can you talk with your partner about patterns you are seeing and then try to describe how they fit together? Here are some sentence frames to help you (see Figure 3.6). Try picking one, saying it out loud, and filling in the blanks where you can with your own thinking about the text."

These sentence frames can help scaffold students' thinking—literally giving their thoughts a running start so that they can just focus on the content and not on the syntax of their ideas. In They Say / I Say: The Moves That Matter in Academic Writing *(2007), authors Gerald Graff and Cathy Birkenstein speak to the power of templates to give students "some of the language and patterns that [academic conversations] require," and note that by doing so their students' ability to speak academically can improve significantly.*

"Can I share two examples I heard from your conversations? One of you said, '**Some words fit together, like** *virus, infect, risk,* **this set of words makes me feel** very anxious.' Many of you noticed a similar tone to the author's word choice. Another example was, 'Many of **these words fit together because they sound** very serious. **The author could have** used words and phrases like *sniffled, feeling not good,* **but instead** chose these words that make you feel more worried.' "

Frames for Thinking About Word Choice

Seeing Patterns

- ▸ One pattern I see is _____ with words like _____.
- ▸ Some words fit together, like _____ and make me feel _____.
- ▸ These words fit together because they sound _____.
- ▸ The author could have _____ but instead _____.
- ▸ There seems to be more than one pattern _____ and also _____.

Fig. 3.6 A Scaffold: Frames for Thinking About Word Choice

---

3. *Use the patterns to* **develop a new understanding of the text.**	Think about an author's: • Tone • Purpose • Relationship to the subject • Central idea

When first doing lessons like these, we sometimes found students who took the tone of the collected words and then jumped into outlandish interpretations that were far removed from the text. To remedy this, have them compare the patterns they found to their understanding of the main idea. This is one concrete way to ground students' interpretations of a text.

"Now we have gathered words and phrases and looked for patterns, and we have noticed that there is a tone or feeling to these words the author has chosen. We can use this analysis to **develop our ideas** about the text. One way to do this is to allow the words we studied to influence how we think of the main idea. We can ask ourselves: *Does the main idea I inferred match the tone I analyzed from the word choice?* Listen to some of our main ideas from the beginning of this lesson. Let's see if they have the same feeling as the words that were used: 'You should wash your hands' or 'Wash your hands so you don't get germs.' Do they have the same tone?

"I see a lot of you shaking your heads *no*. I agree with you. While these ideas do describe what the text is about, they do not provide the same *feeling* as the text. Authors choose their words carefully in order to develop a tone, as well as to develop their main ideas. When we read closely for word choice we can use what we find to **develop clearer ideas**.

"If I were to revise 'You should wash your hands,' I would try to make it match the pattern of anxious or serious words. In fact, I could use some of the exact words from our list to help me. I'll start us off, then I'd like you to try to complete the sentence on your own. I want to show how serious this is, so maybe I could say that the main idea of this first section is that 'You *must* wash your hands . . .' Can you either finish this sentence or revise one of your own?"

Here is where you might want to differentiate your support. Some students may struggle with bringing the tone of the article into their main ideas—not making that new sentence sound more serious or anxious. For those students, aim first to support them in making their new main idea clearer and more text-based. Work on tone can come later.

"Listen to how some of these new ideas really match what the text is teaching because they include both *the ideas* and *the tone* of the word choice: 'You must wash your hands often or you could become infected with a virus' and 'You are at risk of germs and infections if you don't wash your hands a lot.' Looking through the **lens** of word choice and studying **patterns** in those words can help us make our **ideas** about text clearer and more focused on what the text is trying to teach us."

As with previous lessons, be sure to have students practice these skills in their own books. In Molly's class, Bepasha was reading a biography of Cesar Chavez. At first she thought that a section she was reading simply described his home, but then she read more closely and noticed that the page was full of words that seemed to say more about the people, like *fleeing, afraid, struggle,* and so on. She wrote a response to her close reading (see Figure 3.7).

Teaching students to attend to the types of words authors choose can give them a way of seeing ideas within a text more clearly. Words hold meaning beyond simply their literal definitions, and knowing this can provide students with a new sense of the craftsmanship, the detail, and the nuance that surrounds them.

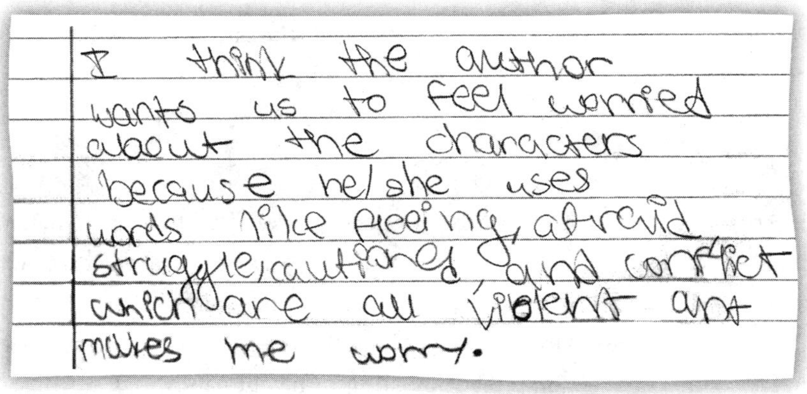

I think the author wants us to feel worried about the characters because he/she uses words like fleeing, afraid, struggle, cautioned, and conflict which are all violent and makes me worry.

Fig. 3.7 Bepasha's Response to a Biography

"You Look *Fine*, Honey": Modifying This Lesson to Analyze Word Choice in Narrative Texts

Narrative is ripe with opportunities to read closely in order to study word choice. Authors spin their descriptions to develop not just ideas, but the mood, the *feel*, of a scene. It is a *dark and stormy night*, not just any night, and certainly not a *clear and starry* one. You can approach narrative texts in a similar way to the informational texts lesson we led with Molly's class, aiming to better understand what the text is intending to say. You can also teach students to go beyond the overt meaning of words, to look for their connotative meanings and their impact on the unfolding story. Once again, the lenses/patterns/understandings ritual can be a helpful structure.

Here we use a brief passage from the beginning of Lois Lowry's *The Giver* (1993). We suggest, again, that students **read with the lens** of looking for words that appear to be specific, purposeful choices. It also helps to refer to a chart to support students in deciding what words to look for (see Figure 3.2 on p. 35). In this lesson, we read a bit of the text and usually stop after this paragraph:

> *NEEDLESS TO SAY, HE WILL BE RELEASED, the voice had said, followed by silence. There was an ironic tone to that final message, as if the speaker found it amusing; and Jonas had smiled a little, though he knew what a grim statement it had been. For a contributing citizen to be released from the community was a final decision, a terrible punishment, an overwhelming statement of failure. (p. 2)*

We ask students to talk about the words that stand out to them, such as *released*, *ironic*, and *amusing*. We can stop here, as we did with the first lesson in this chapter, and **notice the pattern** that all three of these words—*released, ironic, amusing*—seem sort of light, or even funny. But if we think about what is happening in this scene—a terrible punishment after someone has messed up—we realize that it is actually strange that these words have such a lighthearted pattern. We can go a step further in **noticing patterns** of word choice by wondering for a moment: What other words could the author have used? What is the connotation of these words in particular? Many classes have noticed that the beginning of the book seems really ominous, but some words do not fit that tone; instead of *amusing* it would almost make more sense to say *sadly*, or even *sternly*. As one eighth grader said during a lesson, "You can tell that something is really off here."

As in the word choice lesson for informational texts, the next step will be to use these patterns to **have a new understanding**, to ask *why*. Why did the author use the words she did? What is she trying to say about these characters, or this world, or this idea or issue or relationship? In the case of *The Giver*, students have said things like, "Maybe Lois Lowry uses these lighthearted words to show how the rules are so well-known that it is sort of funny to even have to say that the guy was released." Or "Maybe she is trying to say that the punishment isn't so bad, that they are trying to make it sound better than it is."

We need to stop here to make an important observation. There is a temptation at points like these to leap onto students' comments, to say, "Yes, you are right, a major theme of this book is . . ." or to say, "No, no, try again. You are close but not exactly . . ." Many of us have cut students off and told them the "answer" before they get very far into a book. Instead, allow students to hold these burgeoning ideas in mind, to continue reading carefully and closely, and encourage them to revise their ideas as they move through the text. Frankly, it's just what we did as adults on our first read of *The Giver*. The students' first "something is not right" comments will eventually grow into, "You know, it's almost like the society they live in doesn't really believe in people," if we give our students the time and independence to read and develop their ideas.

Next Steps: Extensions and Support for Close Reading of Word Choice

As your students practice analyzing word choice, notice when their independent work signals that they are ready for additional support or extensions of the work they are developing expertise with.

When your students appear ready for an extension to their work, you can broaden what they see as choices within sentences, for example, teaching them that authors not only make decisions about word choice, but also how those words are arranged, punctuated, how simple or complex their sentences are, and even what rules to follow and which to break. In the example shown in Figure 3.8, we used Jack Gantos' *Joey Pigza Swallowed the Key* ([1998] 2011) as our demonstration text, and we taught students to notice the organization of sentences, to see patterns of this across larger sections of the text, and then aimed to develop those ideas.

This is one example of responding to a need you see in your students' work with close reading for word choice. Next, we suggest a few other options for providing extra support and extensions.

Line from the text	What I noticed reading with this lens ...	What patterns I see ...	What ideas I'm having ...
"At school they say I'm wired bad, or wired mad, or wired sad, or wired glad, depending on my mood and what teacher has ended up with me. But there is no doubt about it. I'm *wired*." (p. 3)	A long sentence that goes on for a long time, like this one with lots of commas in a list and then a couple short sentences after it.	It seems like this happens whenever Joey is losing a little control of his thinking and actions. At least once a chapter and sometimes more often.	The author is trying to get us to feel what it is like to be in Joey's head. I think this helps us to have compassion for him. To understand why he, and kids like him, do the things they do.

Fig. 3.8 A Scaffold: Syntax Response Chart

Additional Lessons for Providing Extra Support

- **Reflect on text difficulty through word choice:** If you notice that a major roadblock for some students is that they do not know the meaning of many of the words they collect, then provide opportunities for students to try this complex thinking on more accessible texts. Help them choose texts where they know, or can infer, more of the words. Success breeds success. As students develop stronger skills, return them to their typical reading material.

- **Use tangible scaffolds to support building ideas:** If you notice that students can do the work when prompted but have trouble doing so independently, then they may need some tangible scaffolds. Our colleague at the Reading and Writing Project, Brooke Geller, is a whiz with creating concrete supports for abstract concepts. She suggests that when you meet with students in a small group, you help them "make and take," where students create something they can bring back to their seats to remind them of your teaching. For instance, index cards with their personal "top strategies" or sentence frames, or a photocopy of a page from one of your books that shows examples of notes you make and how often you stop when reading.

- **Use text evidence to refine ideas:** If you notice students are developing ideas about word choice that feel removed from the central ideas of the text, then teach them to use both word choice *and* text evidence to refine their ideas. When their ideas seem tangential to the text, it is often because students are thinking about the words in isolation. Teach them to ask, "Does this idea seem to match what I know so far (about the characters, main idea, etc.)?"

Additional Lessons for Providing Advanced Work

- **Find symbols in patterns:** If you notice students are good at finding the literal meanings of their collected words, then teach them to consider symbolism. After they list words or phrases, they can think of what person, place, or idea shares similar traits related to the story. For example, when eighth grader Graciela read *The Scarlett Ibis* (1988) by James Hurst, she wrote: *When the ibis died, the author described it as a "broken vase of red flowers"; when Doodle died, his shirt was colored a "brilliant red." Red is the color of loud pride, just like the brother's arrogant emotion, which pushed Doodle to a premature death.*

- **Compare texts based on craft choices:** If you find students doing strong work with the texts they are reading, then teach them to start comparing texts to one another. Teach students to group texts by similar word or syntax choices and jot ideas about the impact of those choices across texts. For example, students might notice that nonfiction authors who use a lot of similes and alliteration make their ideas engaging and persuasive. Equally, students could group texts based on similar ideas or characters and notice how different craft choices get to similar ends. For more on comparing texts, see Chapter 6.

Closely Reading Life: Looking at Word Choice in Our Lives

Reading texts closely for word choice helps our students to be more aware of the messages those texts are sending. In the academic sense, it can guide interpretations of books to be more carefully thought-out and grounded in evidence. In a social sense, having an awareness of how people use language, in our lives and in our students' lives, can help all of us more actively create meaning, avoid being easily manipulated, and seek out those people who can inspire and stretch us.

Invite students to extend this close attention to other language they take in, as well as language they put out into the world:

- **Study social language:** What words do their peers use? Their close friends? Their acquaintances? What unspoken "norms" seem to be shared through that language, as in what is valued and what is not?

- **Study other "texts":** What word choices show up in the music you value? TV shows? Internet videos? Do you notice patterns? What messages are the media you take in sending to you?

- **Study the words** *we* **choose:** What words do we use when we talk about others? About school? About family? About ourselves? What tone do we set with our words?

- **Run experiments on authoring new patterns:** For one week (or more), students could make a conscious effort to change the tone of their conversations with their peers, purposefully choosing more positive words and messages to describe others who they perhaps often speak about more negatively.

Studying the words writers use, advertisers use, and even peers use, can make us all more careful consumers of information. It can also make us more thoughtful producers of information and, ultimately, better citizens in our communities.

We came across an example of a student focusing on the words his peers used. As reported by *USA Today* (Seavert 2012), high school football captain, Kevin Curwick, got fed up with the negative language being used to describe his classmates on social media sites such as Facebook and Twitter. So he decided to do something about his peers' choice of words. He created an anonymous Twitter account and only tweeted compliments about classmates, such as "[Classmate] is a great artist but even better friend." Kevin's tweets spawned other "nice" accounts and then got the attention of news outlets, celebrities, and politicians. On reflection, Kevin said, "A nice word can go a long way, we are a society looking for the positive."

Yes, Kevin. Words go a long way. In texts, in the media, and in our lives, the words we choose matter.

4

If You Build It
A Study of Structure

The ability to create, to make something amazing out of seemingly nothing, is a great gift. Think about those wildly popular home renovation shows and how exciting the process is for the people on the program (and for all of us on our couches). Well before colors are chosen, pillows are fluffed, or apples are placed in a bowl for the final reveal, the layout of the room itself is redesigned. Blueprints are rolled out and plans are made: Which walls to take down? Which to put up? Which direction to face the sofa? Excitement builds, not just about the design of the space but about the new structure that is emerging. Typically, these structural choices involve lots of conversations about the needs and dreams of the homeowners: "How many people might you entertain in this room?" "What is the traffic pattern through the house?" "How do you want to spend your leisure time in this space?" The physical space is designed not just to contain those living inside, but to help them to interact in certain ways. The renovation choices reveal something about the personality of the people who live there.

When we read a text closely for structure, we begin to see the underpinnings of the author's intention. In essence, structure helps us see what the author values. How the text is

50

structured is important; it is looking to see what most of the page space is spent on, what has been emphasized. The way an author organizes his or her writing creates opportunities for readers to interact in different ways. You come to a startling anecdote and pause to reflect. You get to a long list of facts and feel a sense of authority from the text. The author moves to an interesting comparison, and you find yourself drawing some as well. Like studying renovation shows, when you observe how others structure their lives and ideas you learn more about them, while you also learn about yourself.

As Sydney looked at the structures of standardized testing, she began to see that there were some drawbacks to the structure of testing in her school. She felt that the amount of time spent on testing was not always great for kids (see Figure 4.1).

Sydney is paying attention to the structures around her—in this case, the structure of assessment in her school—and thinking about how that structure affects the people within it. Studying the structure of a text teaches us to think about the choices an author makes and allows us to see that in writing, as well as in life, the way we lay out a text reveals much about what we want our readers to know.

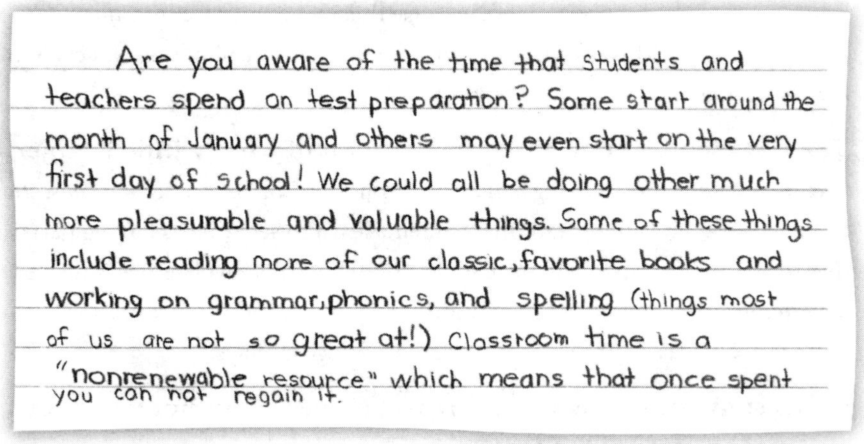

> Are you aware of the time that students and teachers spend on test preparation? Some start around the month of January and others may even start on the very first day of school! We could all be doing other much more pleasurable and valuable things. Some of these things include reading more of our classic, favorite books and working on grammar, phonics, and spelling (things most of us are not so great at!) Classroom time is a "nonrenewable resource" which means that once spent you can not regain it.

Fig. 4.1 Sydney's Response to a Structure in the School Year

The Tools of the Trade: Getting Ready to Close Read for Structure

As you plan, keep your students' needs in mind. Make your decisions about texts, scaffolds, and lessons from what you hear them saying, see them writing, and notice them reading. In *Visible Learning* (2008), John Hattie reviews decades of research about education and argues that "the greatest effects on student learning occur when teachers become learners of their own teaching, and when students become their own teachers." Hattie stresses the importance of reflecting on and responding to what students are showing us they already know and what they need to learn. As you plan for another close reading lesson, consider what steps of this process your students have found strength in and those with which they may need extra support. For example, in one classroom recently, a teacher noticed that his students were automatically starting to look for patterns as soon as they began reading, and so he encouraged his students to do both steps at once—read with a lens and look for patterns.

There are many ways to teach students to talk about structure. We see this as having two main steps: describing the author's organizational choices, then describing the purpose behind them.

Describing Organizational Choices

Three main ways of talking about structure have proven helpful in many classrooms:

- **Teach students to talk about the genre as a structure:** Saying, "because this was written as a *poem* . . ." or "because this was written as an *editorial* and not a *news report* . . ." This involves helping students to think about the effects of those genres, seeing one in comparison to others.

- **Teach students to talk about the location of parts within a larger whole:** Saying, "in the *rising action,* the author . . ." or "in the *second subsection* of this article, . . ." It is important that students learn to see texts as having parts and that they are able to find language to describe this. This involves teaching students location terminology, such as the traditional plot mountain, or terms for genre structures such as *stanza* in poems or *scene change* in plays.

- **Teach students to talk about the techniques an author uses when structuring parts of the text:** Saying, "in this chapter, the author starts with *character description*, then several lines of *dialogue*, then describes the *setting . . .*" or "in the opening of this essay, the author makes a *comparison*, then uses a *long list of shocking facts . . .*"

The language for these different areas varies, such as when describing part-to-whole, one could say a scene at the end of a novel is in the "resolution," "denouement," or even "ending." So use language that feels most useful to you and your students and that matches your goals for them. Figure 4.2 on page 54 has suggestions (Figure 4.9 on p. 69 has additional examples specific to nonfiction), and there are more in the Appendix (see p. 128). Each of these, alone, is a heavy lift for us and our students, especially if they are new to talking about texts in this way. We would suggest that you typically choose just one of these areas to delve into in a lesson. The eventual goal, as with every chapter in this book, is that students will be able to use multiple lenses all at the same time; however, starting with a smaller focus can help students refine their skills.

Describing the Purpose of Structural Choices

Describing an author's organizational choices is one piece of this equation, and for some classrooms that may be a main step in and of itself. We do, however, suggest that with structure, as with all areas of this ritual, describing what you see is helpful only if you take the next step of describing its purpose or function. As you will see in the close reading ritual in this chapter, we suggest moving to a second step, teaching students to describe the *purpose* of different structure choices. In a novel, for example, thinking "this scene seems to reveal information about the character we didn't know before," or in informational texts, we might notice the text structure a writer is using (see Figure 4.9 on p. 69) and say "this section appears to describe the *effects* of the previous section's *causes*."

Those same charts (Figures 4.2 and 4.9), and those in the Appendix, offer suggested language for this, but again there is a wide range to choose from. For instance, in *Notice and Note* (2012) Kylene Beers and Robert Probst offer language to help students locate parts with a clear purpose in mind, such as "Aha Moments," where the character or reader learns something important, or "Words of the Wiser," where an older character gives advice that moves the story forward.

❧ Standards and Close Reading for Structure

Common Core Standards 3 and 5 expect that students can analyze or describe how parts interact with the larger whole. This develops from describing the overall structure in fifth grade, to analyzing the impact of choices and the development of ideas in late middle school and into high school. It is sometimes helpful to think of this as being a tour guide, pointing out how a text is constructed and leading students on a tour of how different parts lead to an idea. You know students are developing these skills when:

▶ *they use genre-specific structural language, such as* scene *or* stanza

▶ *they begin to recognize and describe ideas as existing in more than one part of a text, often taking a moment to see connections across a text.*

	READING CLOSELY FOR **STRUCTURE**

1. Read through lenses.	Decide how you will describe **the organization of the text**:
	• One way is *the techniques the author uses*
	   ⬦ Descriptions
	   ⬦ Dialogue between characters
	   ⬦ Flashbacks
	   ⬦ Definition of a term
	Then describe the **purpose** of that organization:
	• To set the stage
	• To reveal
	• To create suspense
	(See Appendix for other examples.)

2. *Use lenses to* **find patterns.**	• How are the parts similar? • How are the parts different? • What purpose do the parts serve?

3. *Use the patterns to* **develop a new understanding of the text.**	Look at patterns to think about:
	• A character's:
	   ⬦ Development
	• A whole text's:
	   ⬦ Themes
	   ⬦ Central ideas
	   ⬦ Author's purpose
	(See Appendix for more examples.)

Fig. 4.2 Close Reading Ritual: Structure in Narrative Texts

Figure 4.2 shows how one study of structure might look across the steps of the close reading ritual. In this chart we include descriptions for narrative texts. Later, we revise the chart for nonfiction texts (see Figure 4.9 on p. 69). Other ideas are offered in the Appendix.

Closely Reading Media: Engage Students Through Video Games and Structure

We can help students see structure everywhere, but an effective place to begin is by using something many of our students spend time—often huge quantities of time—with: video games. As production values increase, video games begin to rival Hollywood movies in the way they tell their stories and lead their players through events. We can use video games to help students see how the games' creators organized parts to have an impact on their players—even among all that video game action. In fact, some students have been surprised during this brief study, saying, "I didn't even realize this was telling a story the whole time!"

You could begin by saying:

"As we look at the most popular games out there, most have one thing in common—a compelling story that stretches across the game and gets us to invest in the character we are playing. In video games, the same structures are often used as in books—ways of organizing—like the plot mountain, or techniques like descriptions and dialogue. Let's see if we can find these structures in the games we play."

Your goal here is to help students practice the same work they will do with texts: describe the organization of the game and the purpose of that organization. To begin, have students look at printed video game synopses, cutscenes, or even the start of an actual game. Have them first describe the structure, noting that this appears to be the "introduction" or "exposition." Then have them read or watch a bit of the game and think about the purpose of that part. What did the game creators introduce? What impact are they intending to have on players? Even the opening to seemingly simple games like *New Super Mario Bros.*™ *Wii* (Nintendo 2009) creates an emotional connection to drive players to want to care about certain characters, fear others, and aim to win.

With one class of sixth graders, we read through the first part of the synopsis of the popular game *Uncharted 3: Drake's Deception*™ (Sony Computer Entertainment 2011).

Together, we used our structure chart (see Figure 4.2 on p. 54) and determined that the first part of the synopsis is the "exposition," which includes a flashback to Drake as an orphan and ends with him meeting his mentor, Sully, who teaches him to become a thief. The class then briefly talked together about the purpose of that part. First, they noticed that the flashback helped us understand Drake and even care about him. One student said, "Drake is lost and alone as a kid, so maybe we feel bad for him, like it's OK that he is stealing things. Or at least a little bit more OK." Once you study one game together, have your students study others, practicing these same skills.

On the first day of this work, Jorge, a sixth grader, noticed that the structure of the game he was studying, *Halo 4* (Microsoft Studios 2012), was similar to a book he just read, *Harry Potter and the Sorcerer's Stone* (Rowling 1999). Taking what he had learned about structure from studying video games, he wrote about it (see Figure 4.3).

The first step in studying structure is being able to notice it. As students learn to see the parts of things, the steps involved, they develop the ability to see how those parts work and interact with each other.

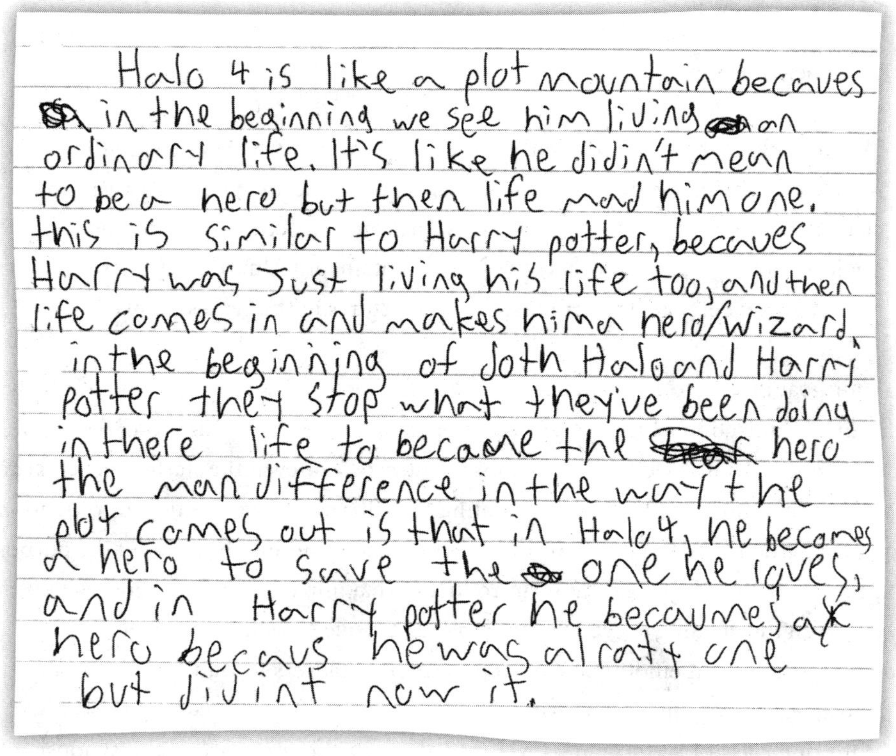

Halo 4 is like a plot mountain becaues in the beginning we see him living on an ordinary life. It's like he didin't mean to be a hero but then life mad him one. this is similar to Harry potter, becaues Harry was Just living his life too, and then life comes in and makes him a nerd/wizard. in the beginning of Joth Halo and Harry potter they stop what they've been doing in there life to became the hero the man difference in the way the plot comes out is that in Halo 4, he becomes a hero to save the one he igves, and in Harry potter he becaumes a hero becaus he was alraity one but didint now it.

Fig. 4.3 Jorge's Video Game Jotting

How the Pieces Fit Together: Closely Reading Narrative Texts to Analyze Structure and Theme

We use the close reading ritual here to support students in describing the structure of narrative texts and then use what they see to develop ideas. For this lesson, we use the analysis of structure to support students in thinking more deeply about the themes in their texts.

This lesson evolved over a lot of trial and error, and, in particular, with the support of Brian Sweeney and his tenth graders in Queens, NY. Brian decided to demonstrate this lesson with a text his students were just finishing studying together, *A Tale of Two Cities* (1859), the Charles Dickens novel that takes place during the lead-up to the French Revolution. It felt like an interesting choice for this study because the structure of the novel involves many interwoven plot lines.

As always, your choice of texts, supports, and instructional goals will come from your assessment of your students. With some classes, we have found other texts with unique structures to be equally interesting studies, like Angela Johnson's *The First Part Last* (2003) and Kasie West's *Pivot Point* (2013). But looking carefully at texts with more traditional structures is equally supportive, like studying selections from Naomi Shihab Nye's "very short stories" collection *There Is No Long Distance Now* (2011).

	Reading Closely for **Structure**

1. Read through lenses.	Decide how you will describe **the organization of the text:**
	• One way is *the techniques the author uses*
	   ◆ Descriptions
	   ◆ Dialogue between characters
	   ◆ Flashbacks
	   ◆ Definition of a term
	Then describe the **purpose** of that organization:
	• To set the stage
	• To reveal
	• To create suspense
	(See Appendix for other examples.)

In previous lessons, we have mentioned that you could divide up the steps of this ritual into more than one class session. Here, as an example, we have done just that—we study lenses on the first day, patterns and ideas on the second. We use the ritual of close reading to support students in first analyzing the structure of scenes and then use this analysis to think about the theme. We state this instructional goal clearly at the start of the lesson to help students see the purpose of our teaching.

"A lot of books you read might feel like a roller coaster—each chapter or section bringing you up to a high point and then bringing you down again, only to set you up for the next big moment. We call this the plot. Like the cars on a roller coaster that are connected, all plots are made up of scenes and chapters, which in turn are made up of lines and paragraphs and setting and dialogue and the list goes on. Authors make careful decisions about how to structure all of those parts. One interesting way to read closely is to read trying to see just how and why an author made those decisions. This can often help us have new ideas about the messages inside the text, or the text's themes.

"We have read Charles Dickens' *A Tale of Two Cities* together and have been doing some thinking about the themes we see in this novel. One theme that kept coming up in your writing and discussions is the idea of sacrifice. So we are going to hold onto this idea of sacrifice and see if, by looking at the structure of the text, we can think more deeply about this theme."

You could start this lesson without a theme in mind and use your study of structure to help you see ones that emerge. Here, we decided to begin with a theme that the class had developed together. We did this because we wanted to show students the power in revising our thinking after a close read, but you might decide to dive into the structure work first.

"To **read with the lens** of structure we need to read looking for parts—trying to see where the author moves from one section or technique to another. There are usually shifts in the kind of writing, a shift in tone, or even a change in topic. With really challenging texts, we can stop if we feel a little lost and then look for parts—I think most of us agreed that *A Tale of Two Cities* is densely written and kind of tough to understand at times. When we stop we can look to see if what the author is doing changes—literally thinking, 'there was just *description*, but now there is *dialogue*, I should stop.' Slowing down to see the parts in the text, to reread them carefully, can help with our understanding."

The scaffold we will use in this part of the lesson is to annotate a scene, but before we ask students to dive into this work, we want to be sure they understand how to describe the part and its purpose. First we demonstrate, then we ask students to work on the text with partners.

"After I read the tavern scene, when Darnay and Carton meet after Darnay is saved, I stopped. Here is what I think the first 'part' of this scene is:

> *Drawing his arm through his own, he took him down Ludgate-hill to Fleet-street, and so, up a covered way, into a tavern. Here, they were shown into a little room, where Charles Darnay was soon recruiting his strength with a good plain dinner and good wine: while Carton sat opposite to him at the same table, with his separate bottle of port before him, and his fully half-insolent manner upon him.*

"So I want to **read this with the lens** of structure and think, 'What kind of part is this, and what purpose is it serving?' I can use our chart to help me out (see Figure 4.2 on p. 54). I think this part is mostly telling us about the setting. It's *setting description*—talking about the tavern and the street and so on. You can write this down, so you can have a record of your thinking to come back to. You can mark it with sticky notes, or—if some of you bought a copy of the book—you can write in the text, or this could even be a two-column chart in your notebook. I copied this page so I could write right on it for you. I am going to annotate the *left side* of the page with what I notice about the organization of the text: it is *setting description*.

"Once you have a **lens** of looking for parts it can actually be pretty simple. Look briefly at the next section of text below this one. What do you notice? What could we call this? Look back at our chart (see Figure 4.2 on p. 54). Right! The organization of the text here is *dialogue*. We can write this on the left side of the page.

"We could go on like this through this section of the novel, but I want to stop to point out that our **lens** in this ritual has two parts: first to describe the organization of the text and then to describe the purpose of that organization. Let's go back to the *setting description*. I want to think about what purpose the setting description is serving—why the author may have begun his scene in this way. To do this, think about what we know of the plot so far and think, 'What does the author want us to see or know here?' If I look at the second section of our chart, the purposes section (see Figure 4.2 on p. 54), I think because it is the beginning of the scene it is *setting the stage* for what is coming next. The descriptions include: 'drawing his arm' through Carton's, a 'covered way' to a tavern, a 'little room' for just the two of them, and the 'dinner and wine' they had together. As I read, I think that this *setting description* might also be *showing* these two joined together: their arms linked, the small room, the dinner between what seems like two friends. I'm going to annotate this on the right side of the page: *sets the stage and shows them together as friends.*

"See how by **reading with the lens** of structure I can name the parts of a scene and what purpose they serve? With a dense text like this, I notice that by doing this I am also understanding some of the details I missed when I read the first time. Why don't you try on the next part? We said this was *dialogue*. Discuss with your partner what purpose it might serve. Look at our chart for help (see Figure 4.2 on p. 54).

> 'Do you feel, yet, that you belong to this terrestrial scheme again, Mr. Darnay?'
> 'I am frightfully confused regarding time and place; but I am so far mended as to feel that.'
> 'It must be an immense satisfaction!'
> He said it bitterly, and filled up his glass again: which was a large one.
> 'As to me, the greatest desire I have, is to forget that I belong to it. It has no good in it for me—except wine like this—nor I for it. So we are not much alike in that particular. Indeed, I begin to think we are not much alike in any particular, you and I.'

"Let's come back together. Describing the purpose of a part is sometimes tricky. To help, you used the chart and filled in the blank with which purpose felt right. Some of you said that this *dialogue* is here *to show* how angry Carton is at Darnay. Others of you said this was here *to reveal* how different the two men are—*to compare* them, in a way.

"Check out what this looks like in my copy of this text. I wrote on the left side, **the organization of the text** and on the right side, the **purpose** I think it served (see Figure 4.4).

"I want to give you some practice doing this with some more scenes, so we are going to end our lesson here for today. Could you go back to your copies of *A Tale of Two Cities* and, with a partner, choose two more scenes that you feel go with the Tavern scene in some way—maybe scenes that have Carton and Darnay together, or scenes

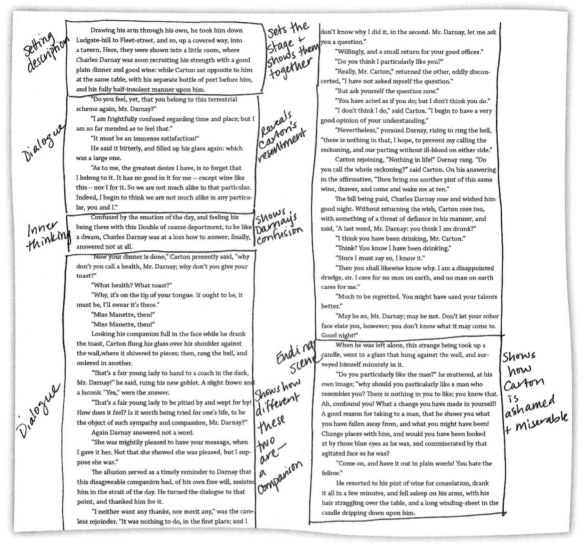

Fig. 4.4 A Scaffold: Boxing and Annotating Scenes

that involve Carton reflecting on his life? Then practice this left side/right side annotating with those scenes—on sticky notes, in your book if you own it, or jot in your notebook. Use the chart to help if you get stuck. After you finish, you can return to your own independent reading. Perhaps you will notice structures within those books more clearly, too. Tomorrow we will look across different scenes for patterns and turn those patterns into ideas."

We suggest you pause here for this class to practice with partners and return to the rest of the lesson the following day. When looking for the patterns of structure within a text, it helps to have a few annotated scenes collected.

When we continue with this lesson the following school day, notice how we pick back up with the familiar skill, briefly referencing two examples from partnerships the previous day, then moving forward to discuss patterns and ideas.

"Yesterday as you worked, you were able to notice the organization of several scenes and think about the purposes of that organization. A few partners chose the scene right after the tavern, with Carton and his friend Mr. Stryker, when they talk mostly about how bad off Carton is and why he can't be more like Mr. Stryker. You saw parts where the author writes character description and that the purpose of this is to compare Stryker and Carton to each other. You saw dialogue that revealed Carton's history of not working hard enough or trying to better himself. Other partners annotated an ending scene of Carton alone that describes him as a man who wasted his talents and is sleeping on a pillow wet with tears.

"**Reading with the lens** of structure allows us to see the parts of a text and to think a bit about why the author put those parts there. Next we will **look for patterns**. Those patterns will ultimately help us develop a way of thinking about how and why the parts fit together and how they develop themes."

	READING CLOSELY FOR **STRUCTURE**
2. *Use lenses to* **find patterns.**	• How are the parts similar? • How are the parts different? • What purpose do the parts serve?

Here we are looking for patterns in the ways that the author constructs his or her scenes and the parts that stick out as exceptions.

"OK, so we have a bunch of scenes that we have annotated for structure, jotting a description on the left side of the page and a purpose for that part on the right. Now let's **look for patterns** in how Charles Dickens tends to construct his scenes. To do this we can look across our notes and see what keeps coming up as structures in these scenes and what sticks out."

Tavern scene (pp. 87–89):	Stryker scene (pp. 89–94):	Lucie and Carton scene (pp. 157–159):
1. Setting description that sets the stage and shows the men together	1. Description that compares them to each other and to a lion and a jackal	1. Backstory that reveals Lucie has never been comfortable with Carton
2. Dialogue that reveals Carton's resentment	2. Dialogue that reveals Carton has always been up and down	2. Dialogue that compares how different Carton is with Lucie than with anyone else
3. Inner thinking that shows Darnay's confusion	3. Dialogue that hints at Carton's interest in Lucie	3. Dialogue that reveals Carton's love and Lucie's wish that Carton would better himself
4. Dialogue that shows a comparison between the two men	4. Ending scene that describes Carton going to bed miserable	4. Ending scene that reveals Carton's idea of giving his life for Lucie
5. Ending inner thinking of Carton alone		

Fig. 4.5 Student Observations in Three Scenes from *A Tale of Two Cities*

In order to look at the patterns for structure, your students will need to look across their notes for a few scenes. In your classroom, you might put a selection of the students' annotated pages on a document camera and flip through them to show the work that your class will actually do. In Figure 4.5, we have outlined what students found when they read three scenes with the lens of structure.

"It is really helpful to have all of these annotations next to each other because some patterns seem to jump right out at me. One **pattern** I see straight away is that there is a lot that Dickens reveals through conversation, or dialogue. Over and over again we jotted 'dialogue that reveals.' Take a minute with your partner and talk about any other patterns you are seeing."

If we are doing all of the work, then the students don't have enough chances to practice what we are teaching. Here we stop and let our class have a go.

"OK, two of you said it seems like there are lots of moments of comparison—like between Carton and Darnay in many scenes, but even between Carton and Mr. Stryker. Another group noticed that a **pattern they saw** is that many scenes seem to end with Sydney Carton, alone, feeling badly about himself, or reflecting on everything he did wrong."

	READING CLOSELY FOR **STRUCTURE**

3. *Use the patterns to* **develop a new understanding of the text.**	Look at patterns to think about:
	• A character's:
	   ◦ Development
	• A whole text's:
	   ◦ Themes
	   ◦ Central ideas
	   ◦ Author's purpose
	(See Appendix for more examples.)

We see two helpful ways to consider the relationship of structure to having a new understanding—in this lesson, to theme. One, using the structure of a text will help you to discover a theme, or two, as in this lesson, beginning with a theme in mind and seeing how the parts, or scenes, of a text have helped to develop it. We return to this second way here.

"Anytime we do some work on a text, we want to step back and ask ourselves: So what? So what if Dickens ends his scenes with Carton depressed? So what if he makes comparisons through both dialogue and description? One way to find the *so what* in thinking about a text's structure is to connect the structure choices an author makes to the themes we are seeing.

"I wrote a sentence frame that can help us, knowing that we can always change the frame if need be:

The _____ (pattern of *organization*) that the author uses seems to _____ (pattern of *purpose*) . . . This adds to the development of the theme of _____ (*theme*) by _____ (*what the structure/purpose makes you think about the theme*).

"I'm going to try this with one structure pattern, then I'll ask you to try with another: 'The **comparisons** that Charles Dickens uses in many scenes seem to **reveal** how bad off Carton is, how compared to everyone else he is so down on his luck and depressed. This adds to the development of the theme of **sacrifice** by . . .'

"So let me pause there and think: How do these comparisons that show how bad off Carton is in comparison to everyone else, develop the theme of sacrifice in this novel? How does it connect? From the start of the novel to the end . . . Oh, here is an idea: Each of these parts shows Carton as less than others; he is not as good-hearted as Darnay, not as successful and driven as Stryker, and not as deserving of the love of the woman he wants. But then at the end, when he gives his life for other people's happiness, he is almost better than all of them, which makes him seem more heroic. So we can end our sentence frame with: 'This adds to the development of the theme of *sacrifice* by *repeating scenes over and over that show who Carton has been his whole life to ending with a scene where he becomes someone new when he makes his greatest sacrifice.'*

"Can you talk a bit about another pattern we saw? Let's try this one, the fact that so many scenes seem to end with Carton alone and unhappy."

As students talk, help them to make connections across the text. You can use helpful prompts like, "Is there another scene that connects to?" Or, "What is changing as the book goes on?" Or even, "What might that say about the theme?" These prompts can help students to articulate hard-to-say ideas.

"Nice work! One group wrote: 'The way Dickens *ends many scenes with a description* of Carton alone *reveals* how miserable Carton is for much of the novel. This adds to the development of the theme of *sacrifice* because *over the book, he becomes more and more aware of how unhappy he is. Maybe it is easier to sacrifice something when you are unhappy than when you are happy.'*"

As students become more and more adept in their study of structure, there are many different directions you can take them, some of which are described in the Extensions section of this chapter (see p. 71). One way is to think about a bird's-eye view of the entire text. While we can start off by looking at the traditional plot mountain, we can also invite students to reimagine what shape their plot would take. Brian invited his students to rethink the traditional plot mountain, considering how they could graphically represent the structure of the novel and how it develops its theme. One student, Neil, thought of the parts of the text like a circuit, that some actions trigger the development of themes, while others change its course (see Figure 4.6).

Meanwhile, Lina saw the structure in a more symbolic way, with the structure of the text as having three main developing areas: "emotions and relationships," "power and political tension," and "Darnay's weakness and personal affairs." She represented these as one of the character's knitting needles, sewing these structures together (see Figure 4.7).

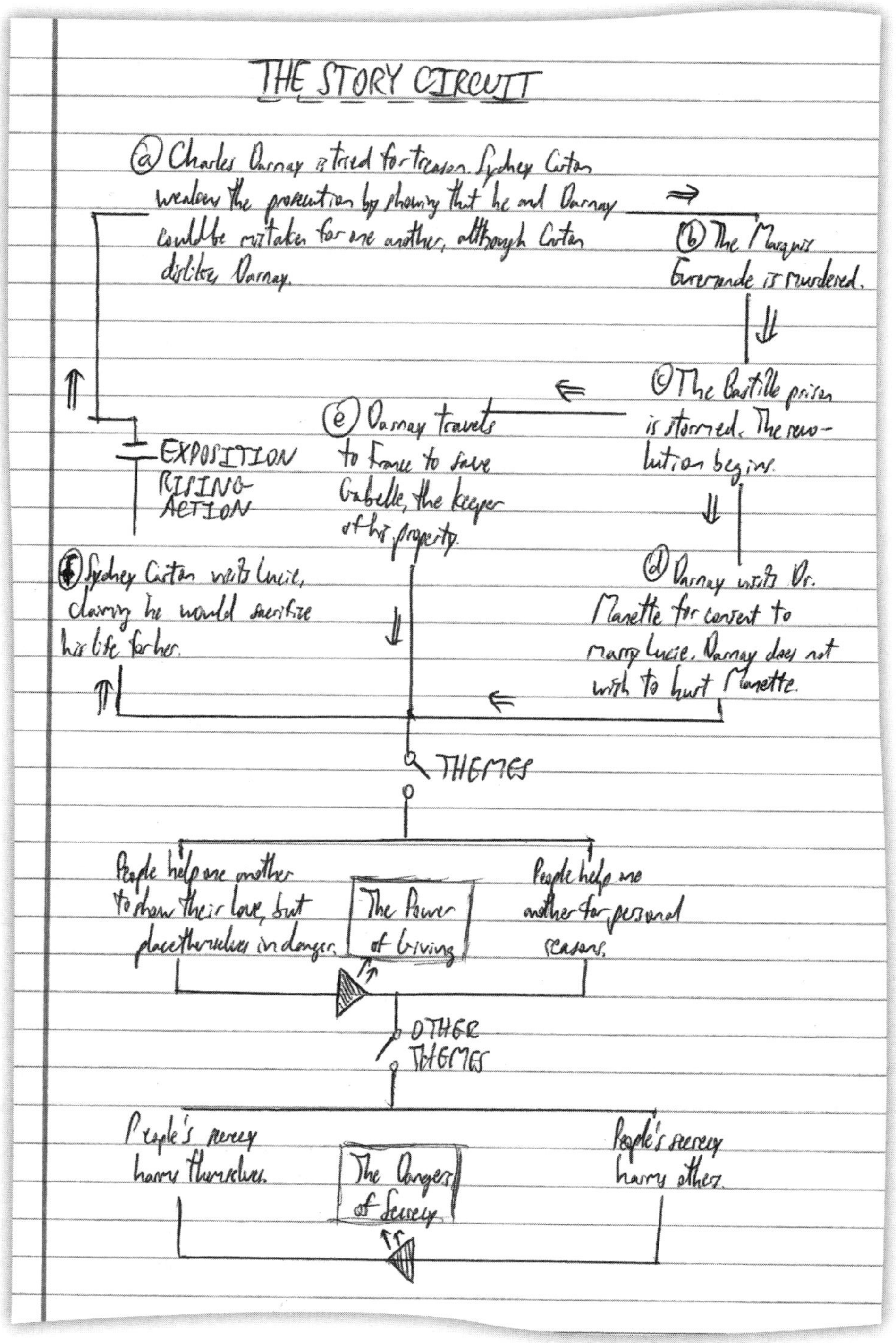

THE STORY CIRCUIT

ⓐ Charles Darnay is tried for treason. Sydney Carton weakens the prosecution by showing that he and Darnay could be mistaken for one another, although Carton dislikes Darnay.

ⓑ The Marquis Everande is murdered.

ⓒ The Bastille prison is stormed. The revolution begins.

ⓔ Darnay travels to France to save Gabelle, the keeper of his property.

EXPOSITION
RISING ACTION

ⓕ Sydney Carton visits Lucie, claiming he would sacrifice his life for her.

ⓓ Darnay visits Dr. Manette for consent to marry Lucie. Darnay does not wish to hurt Manette.

THEMES

People help one another to show their love, but place themselves in danger.

The Power of Giving

People help one another for personal reasons.

OTHER THEMES

People's secrecy harms themselves.

The Danger of Secrecy

People's secrecy harms others.

Fig. 4.6 Neil's "Story Circuit" Plot Diagram

Group 2: Power/ Political Tension # 3, 4, 5, 8

Group 3: Damay's weakness/ personal Affairs # 5, 7, 8, 9

Group 1: Emotions/ Relationships # 1, 2, 6

3) The Mangis (Damay's uncle) kills a child.

2) Damay, carton, and Stryver all fall in love with Lillie.

6) Damay marries Lillie (one child- girl).

1) Carton shares his feelings while Damay and Carton are in the Pub.

5) Damay rejects his power in France.

9) Damay is freed but then arrested once again.

4) Tension (Revolution) builds in England.

8) Minnette uses his power to save Damay.

7) Damay goes to France to save Gabelle but is arrested.

This diagrams represents the duality between good and evil in "cities". It elaborates on the rising actions, because it groups them into three different themes. The plot mountain doesn't show the themes. Madame Defarge's needles are knitting the rising actions into bigger themes.

Fig. 4.7 Lina's "Knitting" Plot Diagram

When we think about narrative structure in terms like these, we help students unlock the power of analyzing text structure—that it is not a matter of answering a plot mountain fill-in-the-blank quiz, but a path to unlock the ways in which books take us on a journey.

Making the Invisible Visible: Modifying the Lesson to Analyze Structure in Informational Texts

When we closely read informational texts with the purpose of analyzing structure, it's like we are stepping back and watching the writer move the pieces of his or her writing around, "Hmm, should I start with this anecdote or this list of questions?" Just as with fiction, we watch, trying to figure out *where* the parts go, *what* the parts are, and most importantly *why* they are placed in that order.

You can use the close reading ritual to teach students to focus on the structure of an informational text and to examine how the text's structure aids in revealing the author's purpose, or message. Because structure involves more of a bird's-eye-view approach to analyzing a text, we suggest you consider giving your students copies of the brief section of text you will be demonstrating with. As you will be teaching them to look at the text as a whole and sectioning the pieces off, they can literally draw boxes around what they perceive to be "sections," or "parts" (either where there are obvious breaks or where they believe there is a shift in the text). It might look something like this (see Figure 4.8).

So What Exactly Is Global Warming?
Picture this: It's late at night. You're asleep in bed, with lots of blankets covering you. Suddenly, you wake up all hot and sweaty, so you kick off the covers. Cool air hits your legs. Much better. You fall back to sleep and wake up refreshed, ready for school.

Now picture the Earth. Certain gases that have been collecting in the atmosphere for the past 100 years are creating a heavy blanket around the Earth. Heat from the sun gets trapped under the blanket and the Earth begins to feel too hot. But the Earth can't just kick off that cover to cool down. This is global warming.

Of all the gases in the atmosphere, carbon dioxide ($CO2$) contributes the most to global warming. But $CO2$ is also necessary to sustain life. $CO2$ is released into the atmosphere when dead organisms decompose and volcanoes erupt. It is then absorbed by plants, which use it to grow, and by the oceans, which use it to nourish sea life, beginning with microscopic plants called algae.

Fig. 4.8 A Scaffold: Boxing Out Perceived Parts

Just as with word choice, you will first need to help your students develop some language for how they describe structure. While organizational structures have some overlap between narrative and informational texts, there are also some that feel particular to each. We have revised our main chart to include more examples specific to informational text; Figure 4.9 shows just the first section of that chart revised in this way. For more in-depth examples and information about nonfiction structure, see the Appendix on p. 128.

	READING CLOSELY FOR **STRUCTURE**

1. Read through lenses.	Decide how you will describe **the organization of the text:**
	• Describe *the techniques the author uses:*
	  ◆ Definition of a term
	  ◆ Comparisons
	  ◆ Cause or effect
	  ◆ Description
	  ◆ Anecdote
	  ◆ Claim
	Then describe the **purpose** of that organization:
	• To present a cause for an effect
	• To make a complex idea more concrete
	• To provide context
	• To clear up misconceptions
	• To develop a reader's expertise
	(See Appendix for other examples.)

Fig. 4.9 Close Reading Ritual: Structure in Informational Texts

Students can then **read with the lens** of informational text structures, labeling the boxes they made across the text. For example, in *The Down-to-Earth Guide to Global Warming* by Laurie David and Cambria Gordon (2007), students typically notice certain structures right from the start. As with our ritual while reading narrative texts, teach students to notice parts and label the organization of those parts on the left side of the page and the purpose of that organization on the right. Eventually, they can just label everything all together on one side or simply make mental notes of what they see, but we have found that for students developing these skills, separating these two steps helps them do the steps carefully. Chapter 1 begins with a familiar anecdote:

> *Picture this: It's late at night. You're asleep in bed, with lots of blankets covering you. (p. 1)*

After a bit more of this anecdote, the authors place a more scientific description right next to that relatable one:

> *Now picture the Earth. Certain gases that have been collecting in the atmosphere for the past 100 years are creating a heavy blanket around the Earth. (p. 2)*

Referring to our revised chart (see Figure 4.9 on p. 69), students often say the purpose of these two sections back to back may be to make a complex idea more concrete. As students read on, they see that the author continues to make comparisons and that these comparisons are being used to help us—ostensibly us nonscientific types—to develop expertise of a somewhat complex idea like global warming.

We can then teach students to **look for patterns**. Sometimes, these patterns will reveal an author's favored techniques or provide a glimpse into the larger organizational structure of the text. Sometimes, patterns of organization even show how an author is laying out his or her argument (see Chapter 5 for more on point of view and argument). As we continue to read, we see that **a pattern** in this book is that the authors use comparisons to familiar experiences to help readers understand more dense or abstract facts. Students have also pointed out that there is a lot of cause-and-effect organization happening in these pages, and that this too is often couched within comparisons to the everyday.

Then we lead our class to the next step—**having a new understanding** about why the authors might be doing this in their writing. Many students often come to more general ideas about why informational texts are structured a certain way, and—for first steps in this close reading ritual—these are quite valid. For instance, noting that the text's organization indicates that the authors want us to understand the content and so they create structures to help us to understand is a great first step. Others notice that there is another purpose in this text—entertainment. "The comparisons are kind of funny," one student said recently, "like 'farting under a blanket' or a 'melting popsicle.' It makes you want to keep reading."

To push your students a bit further, another way to consider structure in informational texts is to borrow a bit of language from the eighth-grade CCSS for informational text: to notice how parts help to "refine" central concepts in a text. In *Writing Tools* (2006), Roy Peter Clark talks about how journalists often use a "ladder of abstraction" in writing news accounts, sometimes starting broad and then layering in more and more specifics. In a similar way, we can help our students see which points along a nonfiction text make a concept more specific.

In *The Down-to-Earth Guide* for example, students have described that the first section on greenhouse gases, like many sections, follows this broad-to-specific pattern. The first part brings you in with something we all can understand but that seems very general—the anecdote about sleeping with blankets. Then they layer in the next part, which is more scientific but still general—the description about how long these gases have been building—but as a comparison to the relatable part. Then each section adds more specific information until it ends with the author's claim that too many gases are dangerous. We even begin to debate the purpose behind these choices—are these authors choosing these relatable examples to persuade us that global warming is real? Is their purpose a biased one, primarily? Or is it that their purpose is simply to instruct their readers as clearly as they can, hoping that with knowledge will come the desire to act. We read on in the book with these questions in mind, paying attention not only to the parts of the text, but to their intention as well.

By helping our students see the underlying structures of nonfiction texts, we can help them see the authors behind that text a bit more easily, along with the ideas they wove into their piece. Without this kind of analysis of informational texts, students can walk away thinking that one text contains the right ideas, or that, as so many of our students have said, nonfiction means it is "the truth." By teaching students to study the structures of different informational texts, we can teach them to always be aware of the author's bias in a text. (See Chapter 5 for more on point of view and argument.)

Next Steps: Extensions and Support for Close Reading of Structure

Of the three ways we suggested you can teach students to describe the organization of a piece (see p. 52), the lessons in this chapter largely dealt with the third, *the techniques an author uses*, because this often feels the most challenging. In this Extensions section, we provide more suggestions, including some teaching ideas for the first, *genre as a structure*, and the second, the *location of parts within a larger whole*.

For part-to-whole in narrative texts, for example, you can teach students to look through the **lens** of the traditional plot mountain. As they become good at saying, "this seems to be the climax of this book," you can invite them to discuss not just the structure of the major plot line but to notice minor plot lines as well. Invite them to look between both plot lines for **patterns** in those structures—such as *parallel plot lines* that move in the same ways at the same time, or *intersecting plot lines* that connect only at dramatic moments. Then lead students to extract **ideas**, such as what effect the inclusion of those plot lines have on readers. Figure 4.10 shows some sample texts and details to demonstrate when describing major and minor plot line structures and ideas about their effects on readers.

Title and author	Major plot line: Follow the main character(s)	Minor plot line: Follow a secondary character	Effect on reader: How do the plot lines connect? What effect does this have?
The Hunger Games by Suzanne Collins	Katniss volunteers for the hunger games to save her sister. The rising action is her preparing for and entering the games.	Peeta has loved Katniss for years, but she does not know it. The rising action is that he also enters the games, intent on saving her life.	The two plot lines are parallel; both characters want the same thing (to survive) but they also want different things (Peeta loves Katniss, she doesn't know it). This makes our feelings about Katniss complicated, because even though she is the hero we might want Peeta to get what he wants too.
The Fault in Our Stars by John Green	Hazel, in remission from cancer, meets the love of her life, Gus. The rising action is them going on a trip together.	Gus also likes Hazel and wants to give her her wish. The rising action involves them traveling together.	The two plot lines are parallel; they want the same things, and most of the book they are together. This impacts us when bad things happen in their lives, because we want them to always be together.
Of Mice and Men by John Steinbeck	George and Lenny try to make a new beginning. The rising action involves them trying to do this in a new town, but trouble keeps popping up.	The boss' wife appears lonely, she comes in and out of the story. Each time she appears, trouble arises.	The two plot lines intersect at dramatic moments; all of these characters want to find a better life, but this ends up leading to trouble for all of them. After the first time the plots intersect, we become worried when they intersect again later in the story.

Fig. 4.10 A Scaffold: Response Chart for Plot Lines and Effects

Additional Lessons for Providing Extra Support

- **Use genre as a lens:** If you find students would benefit from talking about text structure in a more general way, teach them to talk about genre as a structure. Oftentimes, genres have almost built-in purposes. For example, if students learn to identify an informational piece as an "editorial," they can look for the author's attempt to persuade a reader. Built into this is teaching students to use genre-specific terminology within structures such as *stanza, conclusion, stage directions,* and *climax,* as appropriate.

- **Use sequence as a lens:** If you see that students need a simpler way for thinking about structure, teach them to think of the sequence of events in a narrative text as another lens. Start with the beginning of a text, chapter, or section, and think through each choice in the context of the order in which it was written. In *Deeper Reading* (2004), Kelly Gallagher suggests cause and effect as a similar way of thinking about a text. He calls this "literary dominoes," considering how one event pushes the next to take place.

- **Create scaffolds for making patterns visible:** If you notice that students are having trouble seeing patterns in the techniques authors are using, teach them to group these together in a more concrete way. One scaffold is to have them create bookmarks or columns in their notebooks, labeling the top with a technique or purpose, such as "dialogue" or "show differences in characters." Then they collect the details that fit in those categories as they read. As their bookmarks fill up, students can use the collected details and information to look for patterns.

Additional Lessons for Providing Advanced Work

- **Develop language to describe particular structures:** If students are developing ways of describing parts within whole texts, you might teach them to locate and describe particular ways authors organize their writing. Researcher Karin Hess suggests that students learn terminology for structures (*chronology, cause and effect, problem-solution,* etc.) as well as signal words that texts often use to transition through these structures (such as in a problem-solution structure: *as a result* and *this led to*). Karin's 2008 paper, "Teaching and Assessing Understanding of Text Structures Across Genres" (NCIEA), is a helpful resource for this study.

- **Consider patterns that reveal an author's perspective:** If you find students are becoming adept at describing structural choices, teach them to consider more analytically the purpose behind those choices. Demonstrate that as you read for structure, you can notice what an author spends the most time on or focuses on first. These choices can raise questions about an author's perspective or bias. Teach students to consider what choices were made, as opposed to which were *not*.

- **Zoom in to particular parts to develop ideas:** If students are able to analyze larger sections of text, teach them to zoom into particular parts and consider the impact of their placement. For example, students can ask why the author added a flashback, a dream sequence, or a scene with a minor character that feels unrelated to the main plot line. In informational or argumentative texts, students can pay more attention to areas that at first seemed less connected to the central ideas, such as text features like sidebars, captions, or choices made in headings.

Closely Reading Life: Looking at Structure in Our Lives

A major focus of studying text structures while close reading is seeing how authors spend their readers' time: what they place where, how long they make different sections, and what order of events they take us through. Thinking of reading to analyze structure as an exercise in studying *time* and *decisions around time* has powerful connections to our students' lives.

From preteen years up through young adulthood, students' lives are full of structures of time, some that have been placed upon them (school schedules, after-school activities, days of the week). Some they inherited from their friends (time spent shopping at the mall or playing video games). Some they developed themselves (when they go to bed, how long they read). While students are studying what the structures of a text says about that text, they can also study what the structure of their time says about themselves.

- **Compare the structures others give you with the structures you would rather have:** Look at your school schedule and notice how long you are asked to spend on different activities. What would your ideal schedule be? What is similar and what is different between the two? What does your preferred schedule say about you and what you believe is important? What does your given schedule say about what the adults in your life believe is important? Is one more correct than the other? Is there a way these two structures could be combined?

- **Track the structures you give yourself:** If and when you have some unscheduled time (after school, in the evening, or maybe only during school breaks), keep a log of what you choose to do with your time. Write down the time and at regular intervals, like every fifteen minutes, record what you are doing: "watching X on TV," "on the phone with X," "playing X on the computer," "writing about X," "running with X," etc. Do this for a few days and then reflect on the choices you make about how you spend your time.

- **Interview people you admire to see how they structure *their* time:** Consider why you admire that person and see if their schedule matches those factors. For example, you think your aunt is really outgoing, ask if her schedule helps her to connect with people or do interesting things.

- **Run experiments on authoring new patterns:** Decide on a change you would like to make to your schedule, for example, and try to stick to that new structure. For instance, "I wish my schedule showed how much I love my sister. I realize it doesn't, so I think I need to spend more time with her," or "I wish my structure showed that I care about my health. I sit around a lot and would really like to exercise more."

When we teach students to look at the structures around them, both in texts and in their lives, we help them to reexamine many of the things that have often become routine. In doing this, we invite students to think about how our world is structured, the purpose of structuring it this way, and whether or not it is the best way to structure our world.

One example of reconsidering how we structure our time is the annual Screen-Free Week. Originally called TV-Turnoff Week in the late 1990s, Screen-Free Week encourages us to reflect upon how we use our time and to try something new, by reducing how much time we spend with TV, smartphones, and the Internet. One middle school in Wisconsin, for example, encouraged staff and students to sign a screen-free pledge for the week and organized after-school activities to promote social activities and fitness. In a local newspaper, the school's counselor was quoted as saying, "I see students at lunch who are playing games on their phones during their social break time. It's important for kids to have other outlets and connect with other students, so this will be a good way to build community in our school by doing some healthy things" (Kisbert-Smith 2013). By changing the structure of how we use our time, schools and community groups are finding out how much joy there is to be had in the simple pleasures of conversation, creativity, and cooperation.

By closely studying the structures in the texts we read, the media we follow, and even in our daily lives, we can support our students in seeing how deeply structure affects our point of view.

5

Through Your Eyes
A Study of Point of View and Argument

Everyday life is an interaction of points of view. Sometimes these interactions pass by virtually unnoticed, like when you find yourself compelled to buy the newest cell phone but suddenly stop and ask yourself, "Do I even need this thing?" and then realize that the latest ad campaign had convinced you of something without you really knowing it. Sometimes these interactions with others are overt and deeply felt, like when an emotional argument breaks out over why your father won't quit smoking even though his health is failing—you only see your desire for him to be OK, he only sees his independence. Then there are those times when these sorts of interactions feel triumphant—like when you make your case, as you do every year at the Thanksgiving table, about some political issue, and finally—after years of trying—see the look of "hmm, you may be right" on your uncle's face.

Advertising, media, novels, and even the people we love, often aim to influence our opinions or tug at our emotions. We see the ritual of close reading not just as a method of doing the academic work of looking closely at text evidence, word choice, and structure, but as an opportunity to bring those practices together, to empower our students to see the subtle messages in texts and in their lives, to help them be strong and capable consumers of ideas and reflective, caring members of society.

One large, multiyear study suggested that many students graduate without being able to distinguish facts from the influence of carefully designed opinions, public relations, or political spin (Arum and Roksa 2010). We believe educators can help change this. We want our students to be able to recognize the points of view and arguments in texts and in life—to see when they are happening and to actively engage them. We want our students to listen to those points of view and arguments with an open mind—to truly listen to what other people believe and respectfully take in or question what they are saying. We also want our students to live with the confidence of trusting themselves to make sound judgments, to make sense of the world, and to take risks. Reading closely in this way can give our students a healthy dose of empowered skepticism while also helping them to have a more open mind.

Take ninth grader Emma, who carried this thinking about argument in texts to her thinking about the positions she takes in her life. She wrote a response to one such position: her mother's insistence on determining which movies are appropriate for Emma and Emma's own belief that she can make those decisions herself. Emma thinks about both sides, weighing each carefully (see Figure 5.1).

Emma knows that when we are hearing other people's arguments, especially ones with which we disagree, it is important to focus our energies on identifying others' point of view and understanding their argument, before critiquing it. It is only by looking at the strength of arguments, that we can talk back to them with our own well-reasoned ideas.

My mom and I always argue about what movies I am allowed to watch. I'm 17, but she still insists on reading movie summaries and parent reviews to determine whether or not she thinks a movie is appropriate for me. I do believe this is an important argument, especially at a time when graphic content is so casually slipped into all forms of media and broadcast to everyone, regardless of age. I believe I am old enough to handle this profanity, violence and other explicit content because I have been exposed to it for so many years and, sadly, I am able to ignore it as background noise. My mother wants to believe that she still has my best interests at heart, as I am caught between the innocence of childhood and the somewhat diminished naiveté of adulthood. We both have valid points, but in the end my mother usually wins. Because, well, she's my mom, and she's always right☺.

Fig. 5.1 Emma's Response to a Family Disagreement

The Tools of the Trade: Getting Ready to Close Read for Point of View and Argument

In this chapter, and in the two that follow, we want to show students how they can take the skills of the earlier chapters—reading closely for text evidence (Chapter 2), word choice (Chapter 3), and structure (Chapter 4)—and use them in concert as they read a text. If you haven't worked with students on these foundational skills, you might wish to go back to those chapters before beginning this study of close reading to analyze point of view and argument. Alternatively, you could move ahead with the work of this chapter and keep those beginning skills in mind, assessing if your students have difficulty in a particular area and then using the suggested teaching in those chapters as fix-up strategies, as the need arises. With either approach, do keep your eyes open for how students are using those skills. It is difficult to analyze the point of view of a character if you do not think through the evidence of the text. It is also not easy to evaluate an editorial's argument if you are not attuned to the nuances of the words chosen and their implications for meaning. The work in this chapter, then, is inherently more advanced than in the earlier chapters.

When turning to our close reading ritual for point of view and argument, we see this ability, in part, as being able to identify the anatomy of an argument—the parts, or structure, that make the claim. This involves knowing some of the terminology that goes along with argument, such as being able to say, "Do you have any *evidence* to back up your point?" or "What *reasons* do you have to support that *claim*?" We also find it helpful to teach students to look at *how* that point of view or argument is made and to use language that describes what makes it successfully compelling and persuasive, or what detracts from that. Looking at an advertisement and noticing, "They are really trying to *appeal to my emotions*," or "I think that car is really a *metaphor* for freedom."

To help students in this endeavor, we return to our three-step close reading ritual, though one shift we propose is that students use two lenses when reading for argument—one for the ideas of the text and one for the techniques the author uses. In general, the work students do should feel familiar, even though the lenses and ideas will have changed (see Figure 5.2).

Closely Reading Media: Engage Students Through Evaluating Arguments in Political Commentary

There are so many arguments that our students react strongly to, just think about what controversial issues are in your community right at this moment. In this study, you can build

	READING CLOSELY FOR **POINT OF VIEW AND ARGUMENT IN INFORMATIONAL TEXTS**
1. Read through lenses.	Lens #1: What is the point of view/argument? • Ideas or claims • Reasons the claim is right • Evidence supporting the reasons • Counterargument Lens #2: What makes the point of view/argument persuasive? • Text evidence • Word choice • Structure (*See Appendix for more examples.*)
2. *Use lenses to* **find patterns.**	• Which points of view/ideas are repeated? • What technique does the author use to make his or her point of view/argument? • What sticks out as different or unusual in the text?
3. *Use the patterns to* **develop a new understanding of the text.**	Validity and strength of the argument: • Central idea or claim • Most/least persuasive parts • How well-supported • Effective or ineffective parts (*See Appendix for more examples.*)

Fig. 5.2 Close Reading Ritual: Point of View or Argument in Informational Texts

℘ Standards and Close Reading for Point of View and Argument

The CCSS expect that students can identify a point of view in a text and how it "shapes the content and style" of that piece (R.6). This is quite similar to the work of another standard, which expects that students can describe the argument a text is making and evaluate how well that argument is formed (R.8). Both standards ask students not just to look at the author's craft, but to think more about the steps that went into developing a text—"How did these authors form their argument?" or "What influence did their point of view have on each of their decisions?" You know students are developing these skills when:

▸ *they begin to talk more about strengths: "this section is weaker than . . ."*
▸ *they support their thinking through foundational close reading skills (text evidence, word choice, and structure).*

on adolescent's inherent drive to be "right" and in turn help them to listen more carefully to the point of view of others.

Political issue ads and commentaries lend themselves to this study, partly because they are presenting an argument ("Vote for this person!" or "Tell congress to pass this law!"), and partly because their logic is not always perfectly sound. With your class, you could watch a few ads or cable news commentaries—from different sides of an issue—and then ask students to pick one to critique. We chose two clips surrounding an issue in New York City: Mayor Michael Bloomberg wanted to ban the sale of sugary drinks over sixteen ounces in response to the rising health-care costs associated with obesity.

We began by showing this clip from his interview on a cable news channel (MSNBC, May 31, 2012). In the clip, Mayor Bloomberg outlines his case for banning large sugary drinks. Then we showed a second video that took an opposing view. We chose this clip because it takes a side that most students agree with, even though it appears to lay out a weaker argument that's full of inaccuracies and emotional appeals. We showed this clip, posted online by Lee Doren of *How the World Works* (Take this Bloomberg!!, YouTube, May 31, 2012), which outlines an argument against banning these drinks.

By purposefully choosing a point of view that matches your students', although it's built upon a weak argument, you can offer powerful practice in seeing faults in an argument and moving beyond one's own beliefs.

During a lesson like this we refer to the close reading chart to help guide us (see Figure 5.2 on p. 79). For the first viewing of each side of the argument, ask students to take notes on what each speakers' major points are and the evidence they give to support those points. Scaffold this by playing a bit of a clip, then pause it and ask students to describe what the speaker is saying about the issue in that moment. Then rewind and play the clip again. On the second viewing, ask students to also pay attention to *how* the speaker is trying to persuade, what tactics he uses, and whether or not those tactics seem effective.

Some students note that the mayor's video seems less emotionally persuasive but it contains better reasoning. Others say that the second video speaks more to what a lot of people feel, but it doesn't have very good back up for the opinion being presented.

It only takes a little inspiration to have students begin to search for point of view everywhere. Lili, an eighth grader, wrote the following entry the day after a lesson on evaluating arguments in media. After watching a British commercial online featuring the popular band One Direction, she wrote about how they made their case for donating money for vaccinations in Africa (see Figure 5.3).

Studying point of view and argument in texts and in life can bring a new awareness to our students of how ideas are shared in the world. It can also help them decide how they will interact with those ideas, how to listen carefully to what someone is saying, and how to judge if they want to go along with those ideas or not.

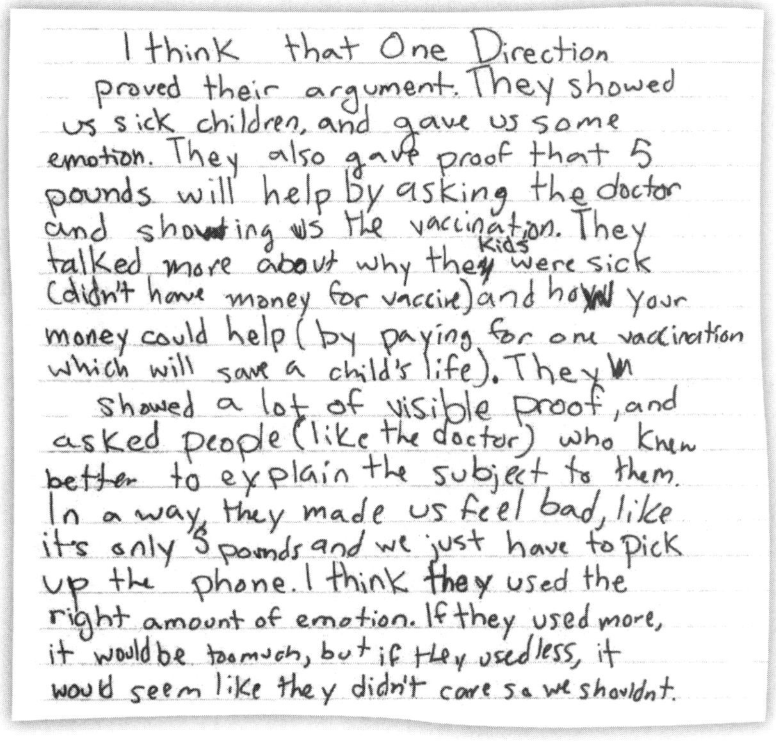

> I think that One Direction proved their argument. They showed us sick children, and gave us some emotion. They also gave proof that 5 pounds will help by asking the doctor and showing us the vaccination. They talked more about why they (Kids) were sick (didn't have money for vaccine) and how your money could help (by paying for one vaccination which will save a child's life). They
>
> Showed a lot of visible proof, and asked people (like the doctor) who knew better to explain the subject to them. In a way, they made us feel bad, like it's only 5 pounds and we just have to pick up the phone. I think they used the right amount of emotion. If they used more, it would be too much, but if they used less, it would seem like they didn't care so we shouldnt.

Fig. 5.3 Lili's Response to an Advertisement

But It Seemed So Innocent!
Closely Reading Informational Texts
to Analyze Point of View and Argument

The route toward analyzing and evaluating point of view and argument seems, then, to have two paths: one where we study the argument itself—the reasons and evidence that make up the supports for the idea or claim—and then another, where we look closely at the techniques authors use to make their writing persuasive and compelling.

A study of argument lends itself to a few possible instructional goals when close reading; most obvious is the goal of finding bias in informational texts. For this lesson, however, because the bias in this editorial is so clear from the start, we chose to have our goal be to close read for an argument's *validity*—a study of the strengths and weaknesses of the argument.

In Amanda Hecker's classroom in Chattanooga, Tennessee, her seventh graders are full of opinions. When planning this lesson with Amanda, we chose a demonstration text that would bring out her class' strong stances and provide an opportunity for deeper and more critical analysis. We chose the editorial "Sis! Boom! Bah! Humbug!" by Rick Reilly (1999), because it is so opinionated and we knew it would lead to great discussions and interesting analysis. When starting off this work with students, we find it effective to begin with texts that have an obvious point of view or bias, so that students can clearly see the opinion being argued. From there, you can use other texts with more subtle perspectives.

	READING CLOSELY FOR **POINT OF VIEW AND ARGUMENT IN INFORMATIONAL TEXTS**
1. Read through lenses.	Lens #1: What is the point of view/argument? • Ideas or claims • Reasons the claim is right • Evidence supporting the reasons • Counterargument Lens #2: What makes the point of view/argument persuasive? • Text evidence • Word choice • Structure

Here we introduce, for the first time, having two "rounds" of reading with a lens: The first round is reading for the ideas in a part of the text—what argument is being put forth. The second round is to read closely for the techniques an author uses, which draws upon students' prior

Falling in Love with Close Reading

knowledge from the other lessons in this book. To make this strategy concrete, we ask students to annotate the left side of the article for the argument *of the text and the right side for the* techniques *they see the author using.*

"Whenever someone is arguing with me, I freeze up a little. I think, 'If they feel so passionately, maybe they are right.' It happens when I read, too. If the author seems like an authority, I feel convinced. But the truth is, some arguments are stronger than others. Today we are going to read closely to analyze how valid an author's argument is, to evaluate when their argument is strongest or weakest.

"Close reading to evaluate an author's argument involves two main moves, which means we are going to **read with a lens** two different times. We know from having already read this piece that Rick Reilly is arguing against cheerleading. But we have to do more than just note that and move on. We have to really think about whether he makes his argument strong and persuasive before we change our thinking or argue back. So let's have **our first lens** be 'look for the argument.' We can use our chart to identify what Reilly does to make his argument (see Figure 5.2 on page 79). Let's start reading:

> *Every Friday night on America's high school football fields, it's the same old story. Broken bones. Senseless violence. Clashing egos.*
> *Not the players. The cheerleaders. According to a report by* The Physician and Sportsmedicine, *cheerleaders lose more time from their activity because of injury—28.8 days per injury—than any other group of athletes at the high school level. The University of North Carolina found that cheerleading is responsible for nearly half the high school and college injuries that lead to paralysis or death.*

"Let's stop here. If I **read with the lens** of what his arguments are, it seems like here Reilly is saying that we shouldn't support cheerleading because it is violent. That is his reason here. And looking at my chart (Figure 5.2), I see that using evidence—concrete facts and stories—is another way that arguments are built. I see Reilly using some evidence to back up his idea—it's all statistics and studies. I'm going to annotate that on the left side of the article (see Figure 5.4 on page 85).

"We need to keep going with this. Arguments often grow and change as the writing goes on. As I keep reading, look out for other arguments Reilly makes and how he makes them. Let's continue, making sure to annotate the left side of our page as we go."

Read a few more paragraphs, then stop and have students talk. Stopping halfway through a short text like this one gives students a chance to try out the same strategy you just taught. (In this particular editorial, students have noted that, within a few paragraphs, Rick Reilly makes a turn to describing, in his words, how "dumb" cheering is. Students have pointed out that there seems to be less evidence in this part of the text.)

"In this second part, Reilly is now saying that we shouldn't support cheerleading because it is just stupid. That's his reason! Cheerleaders—and cheerleading fans—your job is toughest here. Because you probably disagree, it's going to be really important that you analyze his argument carefully. You will have a chance to critique and argue back, but first we need to really look at what he is saying and *how* he is saying it. Some of you also noticed that all of a sudden it's like he stopped using evidence in this part. Reading each part of an argument **with the lens** of how the author makes his points helps us to see when the argument might be stronger or weaker."

Now you will shift to reading with a second lens—because when we evaluate an argument it is not just how strong the argument is, it is also the techniques the author uses to be persuasive in his writing. You can have students mark what they notice on the right margin of the page. At this point in the lesson, you will want to evaluate how well your students are able to talk about the kinds of text evidence, word choice, and structure that authors use. If your students do not have a rich vocabulary for these lenses of reading then they will probably struggle to say much here, and you may want to go back to some of the earlier teaching in Chapters 2–4.

"Once we have a sense of the various arguments or ideas in a text, we can then go back to analyze how these arguments are made persuasive with the craft the author uses. This will be our **second lens**. Our goal here is first to see what the author is doing by looking closely at text evidence, word choice, and structure, which we have studied this year. Then I go back and reread, deciding where to stop, and say what I notice about one of those lenses, using what I have learned before. Watch:

> *Every Friday night on America's high school football fields, it's the same old story. Broken bones. Senseless violence. Clashing egos.*
> *Not the players. The cheerleaders.*

"OK, so when I reread this part, I'm bringing in **all the lenses I already know.** What do I notice about text evidence? Word choice? Structure? What sticks out to me as Rick Reilly tries to argue that 'cheerleading is more violent than you think'? I'm going to jot down what I am noticing on the right side of this article. For example, under 'structure' I'll jot down that I notice he starts by making us think he is describing a football game but then quickly flips our expectations to say that he is talking about cheerleaders. This is a comparison structure. Let me keep reading, annotating with this second lens (see Figure 5.4)."

Help students notice that the strength of an author's argument may change throughout a text; sometimes it's less supported by evidence, with a greater emphasis on persuasive technique and other times it's more supported. As students move through the article, collect what they notice. For the following section, in general, students have pulled out that Reilly seems to use concrete evidence, simple yet vivid words, and a comparative structure. But many students say this is all until he begins to describe cheerleading as "dumb."

Before you move on to look for patterns across the argument of the text, you might consider having students repeat the work they did just now in other texts. This is good work and worthy of extra time. Students may need more time to draw upon earlier teaching, for example, and could use a bit more practice "putting it all together." Do not feel rushed to move on to thinking of patterns. Instead, be sure that your class feels comfortable with the language of argument and persuasion. When they are ready, however, you should continue.

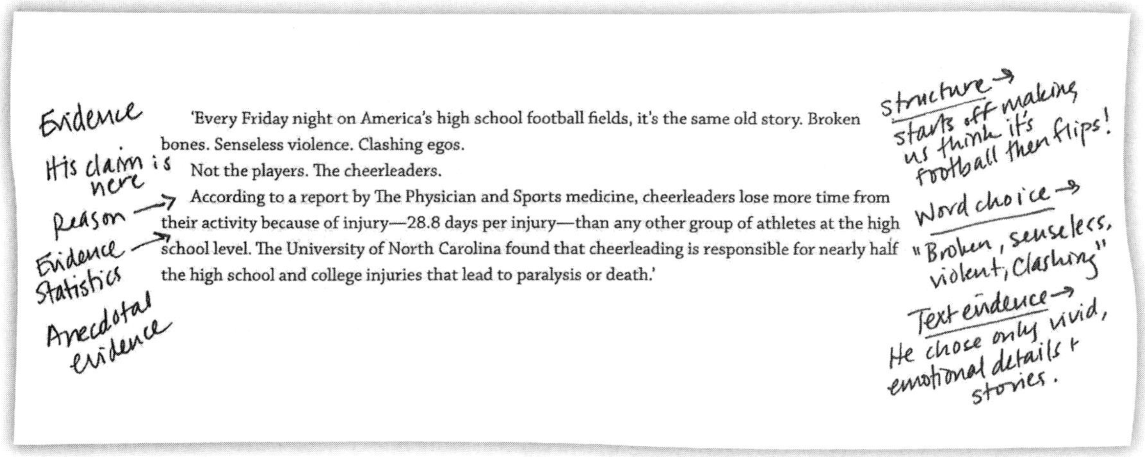

Fig. 5.4 Demonstration Text Annotated for Argument and Craft

	READING CLOSELY FOR **POINT OF VIEW AND ARGUMENT IN INFORMATIONAL TEXTS**
2. *Use lenses to* **find patterns.**	• Which points of view/ideas are repeated? • What technique does the author use to make his or her point of view/argument? • What sticks out as different or unusual in the text?

"OK, so we are getting a sense of the parts of the argument Rick Reilly is putting forth. This is a good time to step back a little and think: 'What are the **patterns I see** in how the author is convincing me that he is right, that cheerleading is "really dangerous" and "pretty pointless"'?

"When we look for **patterns**, we can use our chart (see Figure 5.2) and ask ourselves: 'What is repeated—what does the author use most often, either to make his argument or to make it persuasive? Does anything unusual pop up?' So let me try this out . . . I'm looking across these notes and scanning for what keeps coming up. Well, I'm seeing that he chooses a lot of concrete facts for text evidence at the start. So I could say that 'In the first part, Reilly often uses concrete evidence to back up his points.' **That's one pattern I see.** Could you look over your notes with a partner and do the same? What other patterns are you noticing?"

Listen in on what your students say. If they are having trouble, you might refer to the sentence frames from earlier chapters or to one of the charts you made from earlier chapters, say, on word choice.

"Nice work! One of you said that in this first part there seems to be more than one pattern, that when you paid attention to word choice you saw that Reilly uses really simple, vivid words to describe the violent parts, and that these violent parts seemed liked carefully chosen text evidence to get his idea across. Also, when you looked closely at structure, you saw that Reilly is comparing football to cheerleading throughout this part. They are both dangerous, but football players have protection. And then a couple of you noticed that when Reilly gets low on evidence—in this part where he talks about how dumb cheerleading is—he gets really intense with his word choice. Those are some excellent patterns you are noticing."

<table>
<tr><td></td><td>READING CLOSELY FOR POINT OF VIEW AND ARGUMENT IN INFORMATIONAL TEXTS</td></tr>
<tr><td>3. Use the patterns to develop a new understanding of the text.</td><td>Validity and strength of the argument:
• Central idea or claim
• Most/least persuasive parts
• How well-supported
• Effective or ineffective parts</td></tr>
</table>

The last step asks students to think big—why is the author writing his arguments this way? Thinking about bias and how strong a text's argument really is, gets us to be on the lookout for weak arguments. We can use our chart (Figure 5.2) to help guide the types of understandings we could have.

"There are **many kinds of ideas** we can have about a text when we analyze its argument. Looking at our chart (Figure 5.2), I see that one kind of idea we might have is to think about the strength of the whole central idea, or which parts of the argument are most or least persuasive.

"Let's try this together: let's use these patterns to **understand** where the argument is *stronger* or *weaker*. Remember when we watched the issue advertisements, we noticed that one of the arguments felt stronger than the other and we talked about it a bit? We can do the same for any text and even go a bit further to think about *where* or *how* an argument strengthens or weakens. Let's look back at the patterns we are seeing and think about *strength*. Well, I noticed in the first part that the author is building up his argument using concrete evidence, simple vivid words, and strong comparisons, and I think he does this to make it difficult for us to disagree with him. It's a strong argument so far. Can you look across your notes and see if you notice a place where your understanding of this argument's strength shifts?"

At this point, you could set up groups in your class to begin discussing whether an argument is strong or weak, using the language you have taught them in this lesson, found in Figure 5.2 and in the Appendix.

"Let's come back together. One of you said that you noticed some weaknesses in the argument, like when Reilly said, 'I also hate it because it's dumb.' The pattern changes here: you said he is just blasting us with his opinion, without any real evidence or reasoning. Some of you see this as a weaker argument. This means that you are beginning to read arguments closely, evaluating the argument based on not only the points he makes but on the way he makes them."

As students learn to read closely for arguments, point or view, or bias in nonfiction, be sure to provide them with multiple opportunities to try this on their own. When Amanda's seventh-grade class was engaged in a study of arguments in nonfiction, her students read articles, speeches, and editorials. They worked on closely reading some sections, annotating the articles, and then evaluating each text. Figure 5.5 shows Shuntiunta's entry critiquing an argument's strength.

Closely reading nonfiction to analyze arguments not only helps students study how gifted authors make their points, they also learn how to recognize sloppy arguing that deserves to be called out.

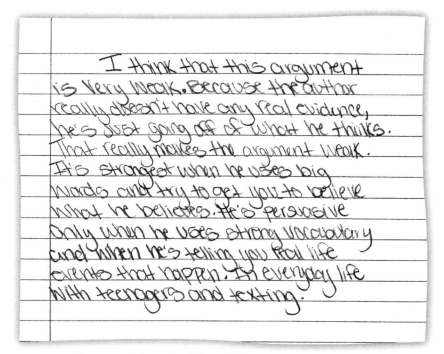

Fig. 5.5 Shuntiunta's Annotated Text and Entry

From Every Angle: Modifying This Lesson to Analyze Point of View and Argument in Narrative Texts

It is not always natural to think of argument and narrative going together, and yet in narrative texts, sometimes there is a clear argument that emerges through the scenes and themes of the text. Some people claim that *Mockingjay*, and Suzanne Collins, is making a statement about the inhumane and unnecessary existence of war, for example. Because of this, we encourage you to try this chapter's earlier lesson with narrative texts as well. However, another way to look at narrative is not so much with the argument embedded in the text, but to examine the various *points of view* of the characters, and how different points of view in narratives contribute to tension, tone, and theme.

While not exactly the same as argument, point of view is similar in many ways. A character's point of view—while not always an articulated claim like "cheerleading is more dangerous than football"—does drive how a character acts and reacts in situations. A character who hates cheerleading will exude his or her opinions about cheerleading through thoughts, actions, and dialogue. In this way, a narrative author is often able to clash different arguments together in a text, with each character representing a different side, or angle, of an issue, problem, or situation. Here we've revised some of the language on our chart to match this (see Figure 5.6).

One way we have studied this with students is by looking closely at point of view in Sherman Alexie's *The Absolutely True Diary of a Part-Time Indian* (2007). In one scene, Junior, the main character, tells his best friend, Rowdy, that he is leaving the Spokane Indian reservation and going to a private school nearby:

> *"Can I tell you a secret?" I asked.*
> *"It better not be girly," he said.*
> *"It's not."*
> *"Okay, then tell me."*
> *"I'm transferring to Reardan."*
> *Rowdy's eyes narrowed. His eyes always narrowed right before he beat the crap out of someone. I started shaking. (p. 49)*

We picked scenes that seem to hold different characters' positions and feelings, often scenes of conflict or tension. Then we taught students to **read with the lens** of point of view,

	READING CLOSELY FOR POINT OF VIEW AND ARGUMENT IN INFORMATIONAL TEXTS
1. Read through lenses.	Lens #1: What is the author's and/or character's point of view here? • What they are thinking • What they believe • What they feel or want Lens #2: What makes the author's and/or character's point of view persuasive? • Text evidence • Word choice • Structure (*See Appendix for more examples.*)
2. *Use lenses to* **find patterns.**	• Which points of view/ideas are repeated? • What technique does the author use to make his or her point of view/argument? • What sticks out as different or unusual in the text?
3. *Use the patterns to* **develop a new understanding of the text.**	What is the purpose or effect of these points of view? • What is revealed about a theme? • The author's purpose? • The effect on the reader? (*See Appendix for more examples.*)

Fig. 5.6 Close Reading Ritual: Point of View or Argument in Informational Texts

listing all of the different points of view or stances they see in this one scene. You can see the danger of a broad look at point of view here: students could walk away thinking, 'Well, the point of view is that Junior wants to go to the school and his friend is mad.' Instead, we teach students to **read closely with the lens** of point of view, zeroing in on things the characters feel about the situation, naming what each character knows or doesn't know, and even determining what each character's beliefs about the world are. In order to make sure students' ideas are text-based, we pushed them to also say what in the scene makes them think that—what's the text evidence? The word choice? Or the structure of the text? Their list (or discussion) might look like Figure 5.7.

By **reading with this lens** and using what we know about close reading, we sense that Junior's point of view is more complicated than simply *wanting to go to Reardan*. Next, we can

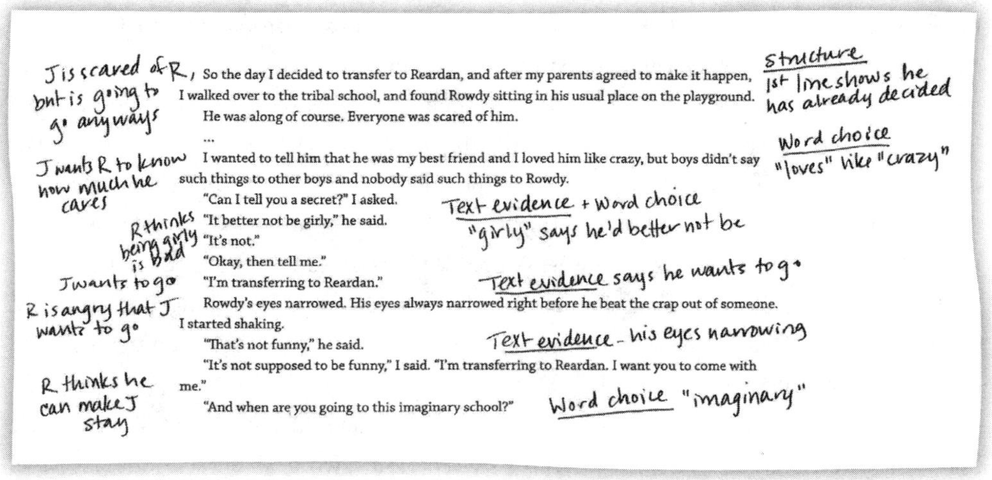
So the day I decided to transfer to Reardan, and after my parents agreed to make it happen, I walked over to the tribal school, and found Rowdy sitting in his usual place on the playground.

He was along of course. Everyone was scared of him.

...

I wanted to tell him that he was my best friend and I loved him like crazy, but boys didn't say such things to other boys and nobody said such things to Rowdy.

"Can I tell you a secret?" I asked.

"It better not be girly," he said.

"It's not."

"Okay, then tell me."

"I'm transferring to Reardan."

Rowdy's eyes narrowed. His eyes always narrowed right before he beat the crap out of someone. I started shaking.

"That's not funny," he said.

"It's not supposed to be funny," I said. "I'm transferring to Reardan. I want you to come with me."

"And when are you going to this imaginary school?"

Fig. 5.7 A Scaffold: Annotating a Scene

show students how different points of view may **create a pattern** in the text. Looking at the patterns that emerge even from just this scene, we see bigger points of view—different *beliefs* about the world. Students can look for categories and see that the views on the list show Junior to be in conflict with his friend. (Junior wants to tell Rowdy he loves him but is scared to, Rowdy is angry with his decision.) Another pattern, with Rowdy, is about anger (he narrows his eyes, Junior is scared of him). We also see in this scene a pattern in differing ideas about what it means to be a man. In this one brief scene, we see many points of view.

This brings up an important point about looking for patterns in a larger text—and about point of view in general. Just as in the informational argument lesson we wanted to carry the work we did in one part of the text into another part, when studying point of view we will want students to do a close read of one scene in a text, like we have shown. But we will then want them to carry this work forward in the text, looking across more points of view and getting a broader sense of the patterns they see. With this book, for example, when students have "added up" their close reading of scenes, they noticed that we really only get Junior's point of view in the text, and that because of this we might see Rowdy as an angry jerk. It is only later on that we get Rowdy's full perspective, when we see his anger is much more about the course his life is taking and the inequalities that reality exposes.

The next step is, always, to try for **a deeper understanding of the text**. Going back to our list of beliefs and points of view and asking why the author made these choices, we can notice the tension that builds, which drives us to read further. We can also use our chart (see Figure 5.6) to help us ask powerful questions of the text, such as: "What is the author trying to teach us about a theme?" Often, these struggles between points of view signal to us that a theme is emerging, and we can teach students to follow these scenes across a text, keeping track of what happens to each point of view in the text. Simply seeing which point of view is rewarded and which is not in a book can highlight the *author*'s point of view. In this case, perhaps it's that friendships change when one person is offered more opportunity than the other. Or to quote a few Brooklyn eighth graders, "Maybe the author is trying to show that for Junior, he is always fighting how other people see him or want him to be." Or as another student wrote, "It's like the other characters' points of view are all the things Junior thinks about himself too. Maybe the author wants to show us how conflicted he is on the inside by giving us these other people's ideas."

In Sarah Mulhern Gross' ninth-grade class, students thought about point of view in the books they were reading independently. One student, Ruby, wrote an entry about Nathaniel Hawthorne's short story "The Birthmark" ([1843] 1987), which ended with her considering how the author impacted the reader. She drew a diagram and explained that Hawthorne made his main character want something that the reader sees he can never have, and that this contradiction—between reader's and character's point of view—reveals Hawthorne's perspective (see Figure 5.8).

If we do not read closely, point of view could simply be boiled down to "this character feels this way, and that one feels that way." This is true in texts, as it is true in life; it is often too easy to quickly assume that we understand someone else. If instead we regard other people's beliefs with empathy and respect—and look at them closely and carefully—we can uncover layers of meaning in their lives and in our own.

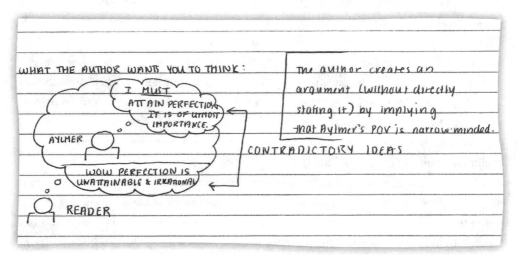

Fig. 5.8 Ruby's Response to "The Birthmark"

Next Steps: Extensions and Support for Close Reading of Point of View and Argument

As students continue their work in close reading for point of view and argument, look for moments when your students need more support as well as opportunities to develop their skills further.

One way to help students refine their thinking is to teach them that some ways of supporting a point of view or argument are "better" than others. That is, some arguments are more logical, while others fall into some predictable trouble, or what is often referred to as "logical fallacies." Figure 5.9 shows a chart that may help some of your students to see where good arguments go bad. Plan to demonstrate one or two of these at a time. Perhaps show how when you read an editorial you stop and say, "Huh? That doesn't sound right." Then introduce a fallacy like "correlation, not causation." Taking fallacies a bit at a time helps student to do the most important part of the work—becoming alert to the "sound" and "feel" of logic.

Fallacy name	*How you could describe it to students*	*Example from "Sis! Boom! Bah! Humbug!" (see p. 82)*
Ad Hominem	*Saying that someone's argument is wrong because they are, well, bad.*	"Rick Reilly is just a jealous person. He must not have gone on any dates with cheerleaders when he was in high school. You shouldn't listen to him."
Begging the Claim	*Starting off an argument with all kinds of loaded language that sneaks in ideas.*	"Why do you think schools support such a dumb non-sport like cheerleading?"
Correlation, Not Causation	*Just because two things happen doesn't mean they are the cause of each other.*	"Because people get injured when cheerleading, anyone who does it will get hurt. It's not worth it."
False Analogy	*When you make a comparison and it sounds interesting, but it is not really the same thing at all.*	"People who are for cheerleading are like abusive parents."
Slippery Slope	*This is when people make it seem like if you agree with one point, you agree with the worst-case scenario for that point.*	"If you support cheerleading, then you support girls having horrible accidents."
Straw Man	*When you misrepresent the original argument, and then argue against it.*	"Rick Reilly says that cheerleading is evil, the worst thing a kid could do! That is so wrong, here is why."

Fig. 5.9 A Scaffold: Logical Fallacies Chart with Examples

Knowing the predictable ways arguments can go wrong helps students be more specific in their critique of "iffy-sounding" spots in texts, and it can help them to look closely for these instances. If you want to study logical reasoning more with your students, Nathaniel Bluedorn and Hans Bluedorn's books *The Fallacy Detective* (2009) and *The Thinking Toolbox* (2005) are great resources. Warning: we cannot be held responsible when a student claims that a homework policy does not hold merit because of the slippery slope logical fallacy inherent within it.

Additional Lessons for Providing Extra Support

- **Strengthen one lens first:** If you find that students are having difficulty with the two different lenses we are proposing in this chapter, then help them strengthen just one at a time, perhaps first focusing more attention on determining what the central argument is and what evidence supports it. In *Navigating Nonfiction* (2010), Lucy Calkins and Kathleen Tolan describe teaching students to use a "boxes-and-bullets" graphic organizer, where students write a main idea from the text in a box and then read, collecting evidence that they bullet underneath. In this case, the box would be the point of view or argument, and the bullets become text evidence, word choice, and structure choices.

- **Use qualifying language to refine ideas:** If students are describing points of view or arguments in very broad terms, teach them to use qualifying language to refine them, language such as: *more, most, less,* and *least.* As students refine their ideas, remind them to return to text evidence, word choice, and structure to support their decisions. Does Rick Reilly argue that cheerleading is worse than girls playing on the team? Or that cheerleading is *a little* worse or *the absolute worst* option?

Additional Lessons for Providing Advanced Work

- **Use author's assumptions as a lens:** If you see that students can describe an author's argument and you believe they are ready to read more critically, teach them to identify assumptions within a text. Teach your class to be aware of what the author assumes is true—for their characters and for the world—and to wonder if that is a universal truth or simply the way the author sees the world. We can teach students to stop at certain places in the text and ask, "What does the author value or believe?" Or "What does the author think about certain groups of people?" For example, "People in power are corrupt," or "Women are in charge of child-rearing decisions." Students can sort these assumptions into categories: "Right," "Wrong," and "Complicated."

- **Be aware of emotional appeal patterns:** If you see students becoming swept up in a text's persuasive techniques, teach them to pause and think about the author's use of rhetoric. When we come to an emotional scene, anecdote, or fact in a text, it might be a good idea to stop, step back, and look at what the author is saying. Teach students to ask themselves if the author "earned" the point they are making—if, in a narrative, the point makes sense in the context of the character's points of view, and, in nonfiction, if there are reasons and evidence to back up ideas. Some teachers have even had their students annotate the text using "emoticons," symbols that represent different emotions, to see how many emotional appeals a text has and to mark places that require a deeper read.

- **Evaluate the ideas in a text:** If you find students are able to delineate the argument in a text, teach them to evaluate how substantially the author supported his or her main points. In *Energize Research Reading and Writing* (2012), Christopher Lehman describes teaching students to think of a text's argument as stepping stones, mapping out the number of "stones" and how "strong" each one feels. Students can then step back and ask themselves if the path feels strong enough to walk on. Reading closely aids in this, determining if an argument is strongly supported by facts or simply by word choice and opinion.

Closely Reading Life: Looking at Point of View and Argument in Our Lives

We want our students to be more aware of the points of view and arguments embedded in most texts. We want them to read these texts closely so that they don't only walk away with a broad sense of the author's argument, but instead are able to examine texts for the subtle points they are trying to make. And we very much want students to be able to do this in their lives as well. We want them to look around their lives as they become young adults and see other's perspectives, analyze the arguments they and others are making, and critique those arguments and perspectives when they find them wanting. Above all, we want our students to gain insight and wisdom as they engage with and create their own arguments about their world.

To connect the reading work of this chapter to the lives your students are leading:

- **Study the people in your life whom you have the most trouble with or whom you most admire:** What is their point of view? How do they see the world? Where might some of their thoughts and actions come from?

- **Study an argument that you have made recently:** For example, asking your parents for permission to go to a social event. What techniques were used in that argument? Were they effective? Could you have made your argument stronger by using other techniques?

- **Study the patterns of arguments being made around you:** What are your peers arguing for? What are television shows, songs, or other media arguing? How do they make their arguments? What points of view are they presenting? Do you agree?

- **Run experiments on authoring new points of view:** Consider points of view that you disagree with. Perhaps it is an offensive line of jokes from a teammate or an unfair rule in the school. Do you sit silently by or do you try to raise opposing points? Do you argue in a way that invites the other side to listen? Practice changing the world one argument at a time.

 While points of view and systems of belief can sometimes seem impervious to change, as students learn to look carefully at these perspectives they can sometimes find ways to make dramatic changes. Kristopher Bronner, in his 2013 TEDxTeen talk "How to Change the World," described the importance of looking at the points of view many of us seem to share—and accept—and began asking, "Why?"

In particular, Kris set out to understand why so many people believe that healthy food tastes bad and are willing to eat chemicals in its place. What began as an argument with his father over Halloween candy led Kris to discover that the candy many of us buy is not only unhealthy, but it is largely made of unnatural chemicals. Kris asked "why?" Why is this perspective so strong, and does it have to be? Could people learn to see their "junk" food as needing less junk? His argument largely began as an idea searching for support, but the strength of his point of view led him to connect with food researchers and chefs, who all took on the challenge with him: to change the perspective most people hold about candy. All of this eventually led to the launch of Kris' own line of "unjunked" candy (and endorsements from major celebrities). He not only changed his own perspective of what he believes consumers should accept in their food, but he is in the process of changing others' minds as well.

Studying point of view and argument is a way to more carefully understand what someone believes, what they stand for. Take an even larger look at it, across multiple points of view, and you can begin to see the sound and not-so-sound ideas that groups of people operate under. With these tools, our students have the opportunity to peer more deeply into a text and to look beyond the page and aim to change the way people think.

6

The Family Tree
Closely Reading Across Texts

We all, at times, strive to better understand ourselves. *Who am I? Why do I act this way? What purpose can I serve in this lifetime?* These are all questions each of us takes up at times. Interestingly, when we aim to look more inward, we often find ourselves looking outward. We look back through our upbringing, across our family history, around our childhood friends, and into our current homes and lives. We examine ourselves by seeing who we are in the context of others—you have your father's temper and his joy of music, your adoptive parents' sense of justice. You borrow your best friend's laugh, your neighborhood's pace, and your decade's jargon. Our features, our accents, our mannerisms, our worldview are all developed from those around us.

The same holds true for the texts we read. No one book, article, poem, or play is an island. Each is a product of its own family tree and current neighborhood. Those big life questions can be asked of a text: "Who is this text? Why does it act this way? What purpose can it serve?" The answers can be found by looking at it in comparison to other texts. As our bookshelves and e-readers fill with titles, we not only marvel at the emotional power of, say, Katherine Applegate's *The One and Only Ivan* (2012), but as we read we begin to remember and connect one book to others, and through those connections we look more closely. We might be reminded of another Applegate novel, *Home of the Brave* (2007), and consider her choice to use poetry in both books. Or we find ourselves comparing Ivan's quiet bravery to Auggie's in R. J. Palacio's *Wonder* (2012) and then see how each author develops her character's inner strength. We do this so naturally as readers, allowing the books on our "have read" shelf to inform our interpretations of the ones currently in our hands.

Context allows us to see things more clearly. We need to zoom out to see what else is happening, to see other examples, to compare. When we invite students to read in this way, they too begin to see how these connections between texts can guide them toward new interpretations and realizations. And this, in turn, can lead them to see the connections to be made across our culture, our world, and our lives.

Eighth-grader Christa looked between books she was reading and the relationships that adolescents tend to find themselves in. She writes about reflecting on friendships and loves and then considers how authors of young-adult novels typically take up these same themes (see Figure 6.1).

Christa is doing more than just comparing two texts, she is allowing the ideas that live between them to inform the way she thinks about life. We teach students to think not just of the book in their hands, but to draw on the richness of their whole reading lives to see one text in the light of others. Oftentimes, looking more broadly leads you back to looking more closely.

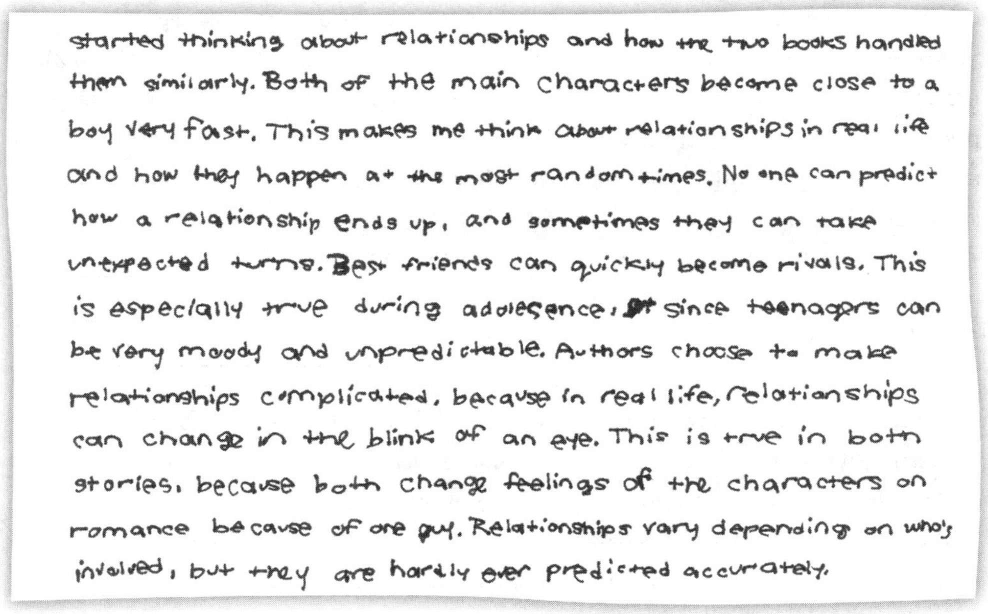

started thinking about relationships and how the two books handled them similarly. Both of the main characters become close to a boy very fast. This makes me think about relationships in real life and how they happen at the most random times. No one can predict how a relationship ends up, and sometimes they can take unexpected turns. Best friends can quickly become rivals. This is especially true during adolescence, since teenagers can be very moody and unpredictable. Authors choose to make relationships complicated, because in real life, relationships can change in the blink of an eye. This is true in both stories, because both change feelings of the characters on romance because of one guy. Relationships vary depending on who's involved, but they are hardly ever predicted accurately.

Fig. 6.1 Christa's Response to Comparing Texts and Life

Tools of the Trade: Getting Ready to Close Read Across Texts

When Robert Marzano and his colleagues compiled research on effective instruction, they found that some of the strategies with the greatest effect on student achievement were those that pushed students to compare texts and ideas (Marzano, Pickering, and Pollock 2001; Marzano 2007). In essence, looking across texts allowed students to see things they may have otherwise missed while also building a larger network of ideas to connect these new texts within. Reading while fully aware of this context, when done well, can heighten the thoughtfulness and care with which we read.

Sometimes we find our students coming to what feel like simple interpretations. A character is "brave," an issue is "bullying," a theme is "try hard and you can achieve anything." Comparing texts can actually support students in developing these first-draft thoughts into more nuanced, book-specific interpretations. To support students in making these leaps, help them become familiar with language to describe what they are comparing. One way to begin teaching this language is by referring to the skills we discussed in earlier chapters in this book, helping students draw on reading closely for text evidence (Chapter 2), word choice (Chapter 3), structure (Chapter 4) and point of view or argument (Chapter 5). Another way to teach this language is to help students choose just which context they will read within. Students can compare characters, ideas, settings, relationships—the list is indefinite. Choosing a context will help students to narrow their focus as they describe what they see.

Now we once again take up our close reading ritual of three steps (see Figure 6.2). In the first step, we highlight the importance of students to start finding their own connections, passions, and studies within the texts they read. Teach students to make their own choices about what texts they will compare and what they will look for across those texts. Instead of always simply assigning—shining the light on what *we* deem important—we must let them decide. As Donalyn Miller wrote in a post on the popular *Nerdy Book Club* blog, "I don't limit my students' reading lives to the books that matter to me. If I define their book choices, reading will belong to me more than it ever belongs to them" ("Canon Fodder," March 11, 2013).

In the second step, we now shift what has previously been the focus of our lenses—text evidence, word choice, and structure—to become the way we look for patterns between texts. In essence, we want to give students *more* independence now with skills that were previously highly scaffolded. Additional types of lenses, patterns, and ideas can be found in the Appendix (see page 132), and suggestions for more support or more advanced extensions can be found later in this chapter (see page 114).

	READING CLOSELY FOR **READING ACROSS TEXTS**
1. Read through lenses.	Choose a comparison: • Characters or subjects • Themes or central ideas • Settings • Authors Then choose your texts: • What other text fits with this chosen comparison?
2. *Use lenses to* **find patterns.**	Decide how to compare: • Text evidence • Word choice • Structure • Point of view
3. *Use the patterns to* **develop a new understanding of the text.**	Have new ideas about: • The lens you looked through • The authors' choices • The messages these texts send

Fig. 6.2 Close Reading Ritual: Reading Closely Across Narrative and Informational Texts

✄ Standards and Close Reading for Reading Across Texts

The Common Core State Standards devote a strand of the Reading Standards to students' ability to develop understandings and perform analysis across multiple texts (R.7–R.9). Particularly connected to the ideas in this chapter is Standard 9, which expects students to be able to read to analyze the choices that authors of different texts make when approaching similar themes or topics. Arguably, to do this well requires drawing on the work of the other standards, including considering text evidence (R.1), word choice (R.4), and structure (R.5). You know students are developing these skills when:

▶ *they bring up related texts in conversations, without prompting*

▶ *they make comparisons beyond general statements and start to include more specific details from multiple texts.*

Closely Reading Media: Engage Students Through Comparing Sitcoms

Comparing things is so natural for our students. Just ask your class to compare any one thing to any other and judge away. From popular singers to books to school lunches on different days, people just like to compare. We can build on this strength with an eye toward what can be learned from these habits.

Here we suggest starting with a favorite and familiar form of entertainment: the sitcom. By beginning with popular TV shows, we can help students see that making comparisons is much more than simply listing what is the same and different. Comparisons can give us new insights, reveal decisions the shows' creators made, and even show us the ways in which our culture has changed over time.

> ## ✎ *For this lesson:*
>
> ▸ *Poll your class to see what sitcoms they grew up watching and which they watch today.*
>
> ▸ *Gather a few video clips of scenes from these shows. Choose a unifying theme, such as family or friendship.*
>
> ▸ *Have the chart in Figure 6.2 on page 101 ready to refer to.*

First, introduce a lens to watch the clips through. For example, have students jot down what they see as "family" in each show. You can direct their observations with some categories of things they might pay attention to, such as "How does each sitcom portray a family?" "How does each sitcom show how family members treat each other?" or "What does each sitcom say about why family is important?" After each clip, have students talk about what they noticed. Use clips from television families across a span of years, for instance play scenes from shows like *The Simpsons, Malcolm in the Middle, The Bernie Mac Show, iCarly,* and *Modern Family.*

When you are done playing the clips, have your students step back from their notes and ask, "How do different shows portray families on TV? What is different and similar across these shows?" Have students discuss what they notice. Generally classes notice things like the details of who is in each family: some families are parents with biological children, some are a guardian with children, some have adopted children. Students also note the kinds of things family members choose to say to each other: and they point out that all show love, but they express it in different ways. As one student said after a lesson, "In lots of different shows *what* a family is changes, but not *how* a family is."

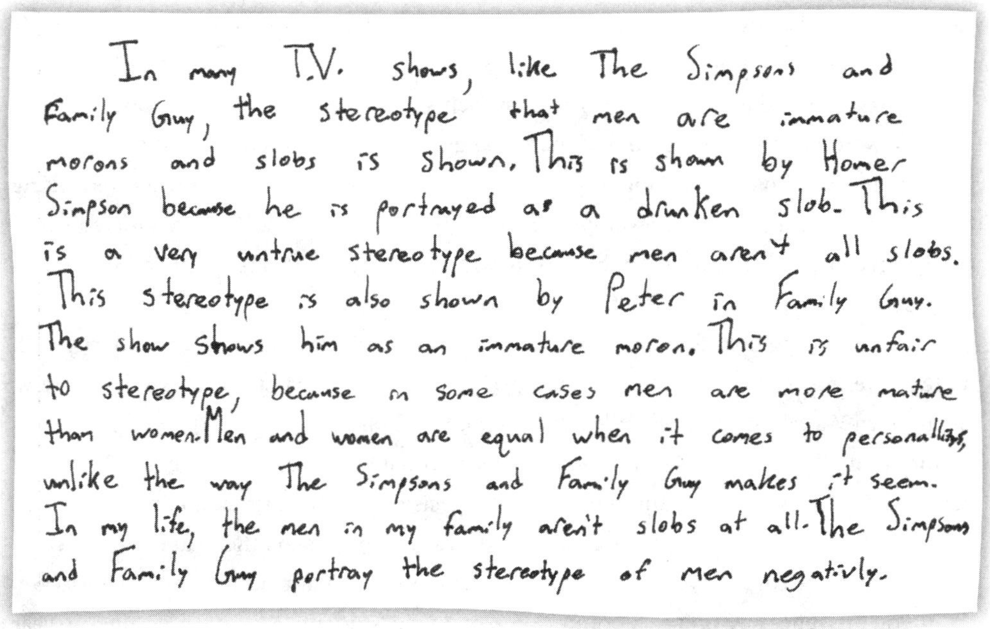

> In many T.V. shows, like The Simpsons and Family Guy, the stereotype that men are immature morons and slobs is shown. This is shown by Homer Simpson because he is portrayed as a drunken slob. This is a very untrue stereotype because men aren't all slobs. This stereotype is also shown by Peter in Family Guy. The show shows him as an immature moron. This is unfair to stereotype, because in some cases men are more mature than women. Men and women are equal when it comes to personalitys, unlike the way The Simpsons and Family Guy makes it seem. In my life, the men in my family aren't slobs at all. The Simpsons and Family Guy portray the stereotype of men negativly.

Fig. 6.3 Anthony's Response to Comparing Television Shows and Life

This is an opportunity for us to teach our students that everything they spend time reading and viewing can be looked at as part of their literary legacy, that everything we look across—texts, media, and life—can be examined more carefully as we compare, contrast, and interpret.

One student, Anthony, thought about how men were portrayed on TV and compared this to the men in his life. In this entry, he challenged the stereotype (see Figure 6.3).

The more our students examine the context in which texts are written, television shows are created, and fashions developed, the more active they can become in understanding their world.

"Stop Me If You Heard This One Before": Closely Reading Across Narrative Texts

Comparing texts through close reading relies on two factors: that students are developing foundational close reading skills (see Chapters 2–4), and that they have read a lot of books that they can draw upon. Some teachers support students in thinking back across familiar books by posting covers of shared read-aloud texts or the titles of stories the class is familiar with for students to reference. In classrooms where students read a great deal independently, students might also look back at their notes, a reading log, or gather together a few of their most loved books.

We have learned a lot by working with students and teachers on reading closely across texts. We were surprised at first to find that the biggest challenge was not reading closely, nor did students have trouble thinking of which texts to compare. The challenge was often taking those close comparisons and developing new, larger ideas about both texts. One educator who has been a great support is Rachel Smith, a literacy coach in Pennsylvania, whose eighth graders worked on looking across texts for new ideas.

When choosing texts for a first lesson, it is often helpful if students have familiarity with the texts we use to demonstrate with. We decided to use a short story the students knew, "Burn" from Walter Dean Myer's *What They Found: Love on 145th Street* (2007). This particular story is of Noee, the "good girl," going on a pseudo-date with neighborhood troublemaker Burn. In this lesson, we open up to the class the decision of which texts to compare, as well as how they should be compared. To do this, they draw upon texts the teacher has used in demonstrations across the year, as well as their own independent reading.

If you are reflecting on the amount of reading your students have been doing this year and fear it is on the low side, then our first advice would be to make more time for reading during the school day. Professional texts like Penny Kittle's *Book Love* (2012), Donalyn Miller's *The Book Whisperer* (2009), and Donna Santman's *Shades of Meaning* (2005) are some of the many great resources for helping middle and high school teachers increase the amount of reading students do. Our second bit of advice if you are worried that students will not have much to draw on, would be to spend a few days having students read short texts before you jump into this study. At the Reading and Writing Project, we love to pass around short texts that adolescent readers have enjoyed. Consider drawing from short-story collections like *What They Found* (Myers 2007), *13* (edited by Howe 2006), and *Guys Write for Guys Read* (edited by Scieszka 2005), as well as more complex picture books, like *Crow Call* (Lowry 2009), *Freedom Summer* (Wiles 2001), and *Fox* (Wild and Brooks 2006).

	READING CLOSELY FOR **READING ACROSS TEXTS**
1. Read through lenses.	Choose a comparison: • Characters or subjects • Themes or central ideas • Settings • Authors Then choose your texts: • What other text fits with this chosen comparison?

Here we teach two main steps as our lens: decide what books you will compare and then decide how you will compare them. This is a little different from earlier lessons, where reading with a lens was reading a small section of a text closely. Here, the work of reading with a lens is more about choosing what and how you will compare as you read. To help, you might list or post images of the covers of the texts you have read together.

"You have been learning many ways to carefully read and analyze texts, looking at text evidence, an author's word choice, and how a text's structure develops its meaning. Today we are going to use our close reading ritual to go beyond looking at just one text and begin to compare texts to one another. It's like when we looked at those sitcoms—by comparing the idea of family across a bunch of shows, we began to see something bigger than just what one show says about family. I want you to have that same experience when you are reading—seeing how putting texts alongside one another helps us to see more.

"When comparing texts, **our lens** becomes which texts might be interesting to look across, and then we look for what would be worthwhile or interesting to compare in those texts.

"We have already read 'Burn' together. Can you also think about which texts you think would be interesting to look at next to 'Burn'? Let's consider the collection of books we have read together this year, as well as the ones you have been reading independently. We don't have to know exactly why these two texts go together just yet, we just need to go with our gut and see what books or stories we think would make an interesting fit. Here are the covers of books I have shared with you this year, which we can look at for ideas. I'm thinking that maybe we can compare 'Burn' to *The Hunger Games*. I'm not quite sure why yet, maybe it's because they both have a central female character? Or that both contain love stories? I'm going to write that down. Take a moment to discuss with a partner which books or stories you think might be good fits with 'Burn.'"

If students have a hard time picking books off the list, you can coach them by asking if any of the books on the list have similar characters to the original story, similar ideas, or lessons, etc.

"You were talking about several books that you could compare, including ones that many of you have been reading yourselves—all are interesting to think about next to 'Burn.' So now we need to narrow our focus a little and zoom our lens in on what exactly we should compare in these texts. Look at our chart (see Figure 6.2 on page 101) and tell someone sitting next to you which of these you think would be interesting to study across 'Burn' and one of these other texts. For instance, is the *setting* in two texts worth comparing? Or are there particular kinds of *characters* you could compare, like the main or secondary characters? We could even decide to make a comparison based on *theme*. Go ahead and talk about possible studies we could have."

Chart these comparisons. We find it helpful to categorize the titles so they are easy to refer to later in the lesson.

"Here are a few of your ideas":

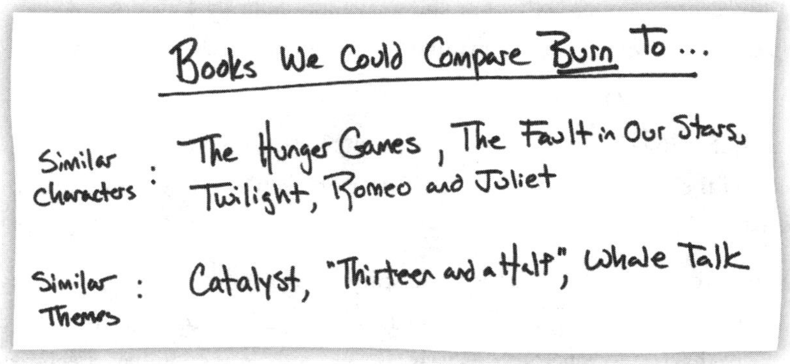

Fig. 6.4 Demonstration List from Student Brainstorm of Connected Books

"There are so many connections we could make with this text! For this lesson, let's **choose the lens of** *characters*. To prepare for this lesson today, I went through these same steps and chose one that you happened to have thought of as well, *The Fault in Our Stars* by John Green."

If you aim to demonstrate in front of your students, then it is important that you have planned ahead of time. We typically have one or two of the familiar class texts on hand, already marked with the page we would like to reread and our demonstration in mind. Of course, there may be other ways to approach this lesson, perhaps more as a class inquiry than a direct demonstration, in which you would act more as the facilitator of the group discussion and support the conversation as the class moves through the close reading ritual.

	READING CLOSELY FOR **READING ACROSS TEXTS**
2. *Use lenses to* **find patterns.**	Decide how to compare: • Text evidence • Word choice • Structure • Point of view

In this part of the lesson, we invite students to draw on what they already know about close reading (look back to the lessons in Chapters 2–5 for additional support). What students typically used as lenses before, we now invite them to use as the way to look for patterns between two texts, noting the similarities and differences between them. Notice that when comparing texts, it is while looking for patterns that we actually read closely, which is a shift from earlier lessons.

"As we now begin to compare these texts through the lens of 'characters,' we will want to be on the **lookout for the patterns** we see in the way the authors write their characters. A good way to get started is to pick some kind of information to notice, probably one of the ways we have read closely before. Looking at our chart again (see Figure 6.2 on page 101), reminds us of the lenses we have used, which we can now use to **look for patterns**. For example, we might look at how the narrators of both texts use text evidence to describe the characters. Let's examine the main male characters: Burn in *What They Found* and Gus in *The Fault in Our Stars*, specifically, what **text evidence** the authors use to describe these characters.

"I reread that scene where Walter Dean Myers describes Burn, when Noee first sees him in the barbershop, and made this list of text evidence:

- *dark eyes*
- *chiseled brown face*
- *a thug*
- *someone everyone feared*
- *good-looking*
- *anything might set him off*
- *sat quietly watching Noee cut Sue Ellen's hair*
- *smiled at Noee when she looked at him in the mirror.*

"OK, so now let's try this on a scene in our other book. I already brought *The Fault in Our Stars* with me and have marked a scene where Gus and Hazel meet in the support group for the first time. I am going to project this page. Could you look up here and, with a partner, look for text evidence—just as we did with 'Burn.'"

As students work, collect what they are finding. Listen to be sure students are finding text evidence to compare, for instance, if they begin to describe Hazel have them look back at your list and think, "what patterns am I looking for?" Have the class come back together and look at the list you compiled.

"Here are the details you found in this scene that describes Gus:

- *hot*
- *staring at Hazel through the start of the meeting*
- *blue eyes you could almost see through they were so blue*
- *voice low and smoky*
- *smiled with the corner of his mouth*
- *didn't say much in the large group*
- *when he does talk he flirts with Hazel*
- *when he speaks he sounds very smart.*

"So now we can look **across these texts for patterns** and compare and contrast them. Let's try it together."

In Chapter 2, we used a coding system as a scaffold to help students see patterns across details. Here, perhaps, you can suggest that students create their own system to look for comparisons, such as they might decide to circle the details that go with the boys' appearance and put a square around those details that deal with their personalities. If your students do not need this assistance, however, let them work without it. For this lesson, we demonstrate without the scaffold.

"In both texts, the love interests are described as being very attractive. Both are described as quiet or brooding or choosing not to say much, and both are looking intently at the girl who likes them. What is different is that Burn is also described as being dangerous—anything might set him off, whereas Gus seems to be nonthreatening, or at least nonthreatening in his actions—he does seem to have a biting wit."

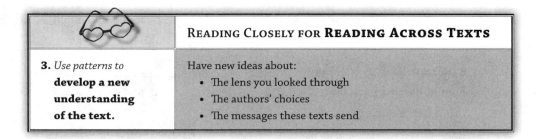

| **3.** *Use patterns to* **develop a new understanding of the text.** | Have new ideas about:
• The lens you looked through
• The authors' choices
• The messages these texts send |

Lastly, we use these patterns to develop new ideas about both texts.

"Looking between texts can help us **have new ideas** about both. There are lots of kinds of ideas I can try to find (see Figure 6.2), but for today let's pay attention to the messages this text might be sending. For example, a pattern is that both authors describe their main male character as sort of intensely staring at the person they like. Also, both characters are quiet or mostly keep to themselves. So I can ask myself: '**What message** does this pattern seem to be sending?' The main male character in each text is the love interest, and these are scenes where the guy is trying to get a girl's attention. So **what are these books teaching us** about how to get a love interest's attention, or what it means to be an intense, brooding kind of guy?"

We are asking students to do most of the thinking here because, again, we want this lesson to put more of the responsibility for processing on them—and it allows us to see what they are drawing on and where they still have difficulty. If, however, your class needs more support, then you can stop to model answering these questions yourself. Then give students a new scenario to consider, such as "Why do both books emphasize the male characters' physical attractiveness? What message does that send?"

"Let's come back together. One group said that it seems like both of these books are saying that being a brooding, intense guy is the best way to show someone you are interested in them. That seems true in these books—it is **a message** they have in common.

"The best part of comparing something is not to say what is the same, but to notice the little differences between them. So we have this similar idea—that the male love interest is kind of brooding at the beginning. Here is a sentence frame that might help us to do some of this work. What if we try something like this:

Both texts have in common _____. **But some differences are that** _____. **This makes me think** _____.

"Let me try this. OK, so **'Both texts have in common** that the brooding main male character gets the girl's attention. **But some differences are that** in *The Fault in Our Stars*, Gus has a quick wit and becomes outwardly romantic with Hazel, but in 'Burn,' the main character is quiet, tough, and not so affectionate. **This makes me think** . . . Hmm. I am feeling a little stuck.' On this chart (see Figure 6.2), we see that you could have ideas about the lens you looked through—characters, or the author, or messages the text is sending. So let me try that first one, having new ideas about the characters.

"One thing that really stands out to me is how Gus is outwardly affectionate, but Burn keeps to himself more. I think there is something in that. As I am developing a new idea, I could go back to those scenes and look at them once more, look for text evidence to help me think more about these characters. As I look back at the scene with Burn, I notice how he does most of his communicating through his eyes. In the scene with Gus, he communicates through expressions as well, but also through the things he says. Hmm, now I am onto something.

"I can finish my sentence now: **'This makes me think** that both characters have taken on a personality, a persona almost. Burn is considered tough, so he hides his emotions more and doesn't say much. Gus is considered clever, so he might wait to speak until he finds a connection with someone who gets him. I think both of them feel alone a lot.' Thinking of 'Burn' in the context of *The Fault in Our Stars*, I feel like we are seeing things that we didn't see the first time. I think I'm getting to know these characters a lot more.

"Turn and talk one last time with your partner, what additional insights are you having? What details are really popping out to you more than before, now that we are looking across two texts?"

While we could end this lesson here and ask students to adopt this sentence frame right away to use with their own texts, we chose to have them talk one last time so we could listen for their understanding, as well as any difficulties they were having. As students talk, some naturally begin to recall other texts with similar messages. When they do, refer back to the sentence frame and the way you carefully selected and considered text evidence.

"While you were talking, many of you jumped to other details. Like one group was saying that it's interesting how, in both books, it is the male's physical appearance that the girls really go for. But then Gus is also described as being attractive for his cleverness, whereas Burn is described as being mysterious. Another group noticed that lots of young-adult books seem to have these intense, quiet male leads— Edward in *Twilight*, Gale in *The Hunger Games*—and that you found that kind of strange, now that you really thought about it. Why are so many guys in books like this? In literary discussions, people sometimes refer to patterns of types of characters as being 'archetypal.' I think we just found a young-adult archetypal character: the brooding male lead."

We have tended to find that by the end of this lesson, many students are in fact already making comparisons to the books they are reading and are thinking about the titles in their reading history as parts of the bigger world of literature. They may choose a different lens, or look for a different pattern, but they realize that the joy and power of reading across texts is not when you do it because a teacher has told you to, or led you to the titles you should compare, but when you realize with stunning clarity that the book you are reading connects to others in enlightening ways.

Students in Rachel's class found it helpful to organize their thinking about texts in different ways. For example, Jessica made a chart to draw comparisons, where she included both books and began listing evidence, trying to line up similar or opposing details, and she ultimately came to the idea that "having some faith in yourself and your decisions can take you a long way" (see Figure 6.5).

Teaching students to closely read across texts can show them that nothing on this earth lives in isolation, that none of us—not people, ideas, or texts—are alone. Looking at others can often help us look more closely at ourselves.

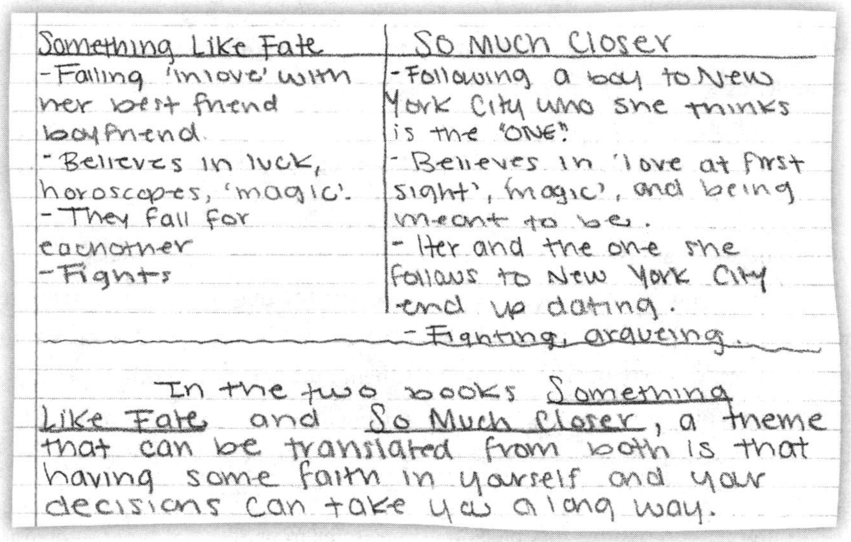

Something Like Fate	So Much Closer
-Falling 'inlove' with her best friend boyfriend.	-Following a boy to New York City who she thinks is the 'ONE'.
-Believes in luck, horoscopes, 'magic'.	-Believes in 'love at first sight', magic', and being meant to be.
-They fall for eachother	-Her and the one she follows to New York City end up dating.
-Fights	-Fighting, arguing.

In the two books Something Like Fate and So Much Closer, a theme that can be translated from both is that having some faith in yourself and your decisions can take you a long way.

Fig. 6.5 Jessica's Response to Comparing *Something Like Fate* and *So Much Closer*

There Is No *I* in *Team*: Modifying This Lesson to Closely Read Across Informational Texts

Looking across texts is an essential part of reading nonfiction well. You read across multiple texts to learn more about a topic just as you read across differing points of view on an issue to shape your own beliefs.

When digging into cross-text close reading with nonfiction, demonstrate with subjects that your students will find worth studying. Super-gross facts, heated debates, and topics that are immediately relevant are all good places to start. Recently, we have been using a few articles about print media versus digital media. For instance, when *Newsweek* announced it would publish its last print edition in late 2012, many people had strong opinions about the switch. In an article entitled "Digital Books Leave a Reader Cold" (December 28, 2012), *Washington Post* columnist Kathleen Parker writes what she sees as the negative effects of going to a more digital world (note: there is one very brief adult example late in the article that you may wish to strike if using the entire text with students). She writes:

> *One can read "One Hundred Years of Solitude" on a Kindle or an iPad, but one cannot see, hear, feel and smell the story in the same way. I'm unlikely to race to the sofa, there to nuzzle an electronic gizmo, with the same anticipation as with a book. Or to the*

hammock with the same relish I would with a new magazine. Somehow, napping with a gadget blinking notice of its dwindling power doesn't hold the same appeal as falling asleep in the hammock with your paperback opened to where you dozed off.

We read this article first and then invite students to decide what text to compare it with. While in the fiction lesson we made the suggestion that students think back to texts that they have already read, which can still be the case in this study; we think that when reading shorter nonfiction pieces you can also tap into the research work described by the CCSS, and that students can go out in search for new texts with a context in mind. Looking back to the first part of our chart (see Figure 6.2 on page 101), students can look for texts on this same subject or texts that might have the same or different arguments. Perhaps this leads to a search for articles that disagree or that present another point of view on the topic. On the other hand, perhaps students will choose texts that provide more factual information so they can form their own opinions and learn more about the central ideas that surround the topic. In the Appendix, we offer other suggestions, such as looking for another text in the context of style or looking across the work of one author.

Often, students suggest that we search for articles on the same subject but try to find different arguments. This could involve a brief pause for students to take to the Internet to perform their own search, or you could come prepared with a few articles yourself. We have used an online article from *The Daily Beast* (a digital journal owned by *Newsweek*), in which *Newsweek* announces that it will be moving to an all-digital format. The article also includes a video interview, which could be a third text. The article takes on a tone like this:

Newsweek Global, as the all-digital publication will be named, will be a single, world-wide edition targeted for a highly mobile, opinion-leading audience who want to learn about world events in a sophisticated context.

We then **look for patterns** across these texts. Once again invite students to draw on what they know about close reading—by looking closely at text evidence, word choice, structure, and point of view to see some of the choices the author is making. Ideally, students will be able, at this point in their work, to look for a few different patterns at once. For example, students could read across these texts **looking for patterns** in word choice *and* text evidence, noting how the author of the editorial describes the experience of reading digitally as an un-friendly one, saying that she is "unlikely to nuzzle an electronic gizmo" and noting the lack of appeal of "napping with a gadget blinking notice of its dwindling power," while the article describes the same experience as "highly mobile" and having "a sophisticated context."

Holding onto the work they have done earlier (see Chapters 2–5), direct students to think across the patterns of words these authors use and the evidence they present. Students will most likely note, for example, that the editorial relies on personal experience as evidence, whereas *The Daily Beast* article focuses more on big, inspiring ideas.

We then move to focus on **understanding** these texts better because of our close reading work across them. Highlight once again that the power of reading closely across texts is being able to see more in each individual text than you did originally. When looking across the editorial and the online article, and even the interview embedded within it, the drastically different tones, word choice, and text evidence often lead students to either see each side's argument even more clearly or, with a little support, even notice that the truth may be somewhere in the middle. One student was so struck by the negative tone of the editorial that she looked more closely for what could be negative in the online article and video. She zeroed in on one piece of text evidence from the video, and said, "Did you notice that *The Daily Beast* mentioned that they would have to fire some people? They make this sound really positive, but people will lose work because of it."

An added benefit to cross-text close reading in nonfiction is that it supports students in assessing the credibility and bias of sources. The ability to grasp an author's bias, to evaluate a text's worth, to identify fishy ideas and powerful connections is a skill that will empower your students for the rest of their lives. (See Chapter 5 for more on close reading for point of view and argument.) Reading across one nonfiction text can reveal so much; doing so in comparison to other texts on similar topics can help our students have a whole new perspective and more careful awareness of the information others are trying to send their way.

Next Steps: Extensions and Support for Close Reading Across Texts

Once your students have learned how to read across texts with a lens, you can teach them that the people who study books often have lenses that they carry with them whenever they read. We discussed literary criticism in Chapter 1, how close reading largely developed through university critique studies. As students become more adept at reading closely and looking across texts, you could consider drawing from some of those past and current schools of thought.

In essence, literary theory says that there are lenses that people can use to look at works of art, and that those lenses feel important because they are reflections of big issues or ideas in our society or culture. By this point, students should be aware of what it means to read with a lens—bringing in other critical ways of looking at texts will fit right in. By drawing on lenses that many people use when they talk about books, we can use our close reading skills to examine issues that deal with human nature, society, and the world. Figure 6.6 shows some examples.

As students become stronger in the ritual of close reading, the types of intellectual work you can introduce them to can vary widely. Each step, as in this case of choosing a **lens** to read with, can provide many opportunities for thinking differently. One helpful resource for thinking more about critical lenses is Randy and Katherine Bomer's *For a Better World* (2001), which details many ways of thinking about texts and life.

Comparisons in literary theory	Questions we can ask of texts	Examples
Gender	How are male and female characters treated in these texts? How are male and female characters described?	In *The Hunger Games*, Katniss is a strong, independent female, while Peeta is actually more dependent. This is different from *Twilight*, where it takes Bella a long time to be as strong and independent as her love interest.
Culture and History	What was going on in the world when this text was written? How does when the text was written affect the story?	"The Lottery" was written shortly after World War II, and the story is about people conforming to violence, whereas *The Hunger Games* was written during the Iraq War and while reality TV was popular.
Money or Wealth	How does money affect the characters in these books? How are characters from different classes portrayed?	In both *The Hunger Games* and *Twilight*, the fact that the heroines both come from little to no money affects how they respond to the adventure in front of them. Katniss spends time making sure her sister will be fed before she leaves, and Bella is all too eager to find a new life with the (it just so happens) rich Cullens.

Fig. 6.6 A Scaffold: Literary Theory Chart for Cross-Text Analysis

Additional Lessons for Providing Extra Support

- **Practice comparing broadly before moving to specifics:** If you notice your students are having some difficulty in selecting texts that have specific similarities, then teach them to write broadly about those texts first. Carrie Tenebrini, a fifth-grade teacher in Taipei, taught her students to look over the reading logs they keep during the year and select two titles. They then wrote, filling up as much as a notebook page or more with their thoughts about how those two books connected. She found that having students just write and think on the go, without the constraint of having a controlling idea first, helped many students more easily find connections between books.

- **Start with successful patterns:** If you notice that your readers begin to get confused when looking for patterns across texts, guide students to reflect on the work they have done so far and to choose from their strengths. By staying within what Lev Vygotsky calls the zone of proximal development (1978), we allow students to build upon what they already know and we continue to increase the challenge as students' skills grow to meet it. For example, if students were able to read for text evidence earlier, maybe it would be beneficial for them to carry that with them in this new work of reading across texts. Have students write on an index card which strategies worked for them, and then have them use these until they become experts in the strategies they feel most confident using.

- **Develop stronger comparison language for ideas:** If your students are having a difficult time articulating what they think about a pattern they found, and if the earlier sentence frames are not helping, it may be because your students do not have "compare/ contrast" language at the ready. Help by giving them some additional sentence frames, such as "Both of these texts . . ." or "One main difference between these texts is . . ." Have students practice what it sounds like to compare things, perhaps with texts and media or even with objects in everyday life.

Additional Lessons for Providing Advanced Work

- **Use allusions as lenses:** Another way fiction texts connect is through allusions made to other texts, such as direct references or borrowed imagery from mythology. While the best way to catch allusions is to be sure students read a lot, we have worked with teachers who have spent just a few minutes adding to a list of "Allusions to Be on the Lookout For." This list can help students to identify when an allusion is happening, even if they do not yet know all of the source material. For instance, a character who rebels against her parents and attempts something dangerous, only to be hurt in the end, often alludes to the myth of Icarus. Students may soon be able to identify parts of texts that "seem" like allusions, and you can encourage them to do quick research on those references in order to deepen their knowledge of the legacy of reading and culture.

- **Researching the author as lens:** When students are looking across texts, you can teach them to aim to learn more about the author's point of view. This can be done by close reading across several of the author's works. Additionally, students can research the author: reading across their website or blog, biographies, Wikipedia pages, and even sites created by fans. While an author may or may not blatantly include themselves in what he or she writes, savvy readers make themselves aware of who is on the other side of the page.

Closely Reading Life: Looking Across Texts in Our Lives

As students look at ways that texts connect with one another, they can also look at their own context as well. By context we mean the people, institutions, ideas, and culture that surrounds us, the things we are compared to and with, and the comparisons we make. We can reflect on ourselves in the midst of our world and our history. Characters across texts and across decades deal with many of the same personal struggles and have similar dreams as we do today; so too do we share these feelings with the people around us. You can invite students to look closely at their life:

- **Study your own personal "context":** In what ways do you describe yourself? Your cultural heritage? Your city, suburban, or rural life? Your hobbies? Your role in your family? How do you describe your personality?

- **Study how your context shapes you:** Does any of this personal context lead you to act certain ways? What goals do you have? What fears? Are there ways you wish you could change?

- **Study this context across your family history:** Interview people in your life, your parents, grandparents, and other caregivers. Find out ways that they compare and contrast with how you describe yourself and your experiences: "What was it like to be (a woman, a sister, a student, living in a city, etc.) when you were my age?" "What goals did you have?" "What fears?"

- **Run experiments on authoring new patterns:** Just as with texts, close reading only really matters if it influences the way we think about things from that point on. Reflect on your conversations with people in your family history, and ask yourself what patterns you have in your life that you now want to strengthen and continue or if there are some you want to now change.

The This I Believe organization is well-known to many educators as it archives and shares essays written and read describing a "belief" that someone holds dear. In one essay, then sixteen-year-old Josh Rittenberg (National Public Radio Morning Edition, February 27, 2006) recalled one evening when he was eavesdropping on his parents talking in the other room.

His father was worrying aloud to his mother that the world Josh would inherit from their generation was a dangerous one. He was lying on the couch looking around their living room while they spoke, noticing the photos of his grandfather in a military uniform, of his great-grandparents who immigrated through Ellis Island.

Josh lay there, thinking about all of the terrible things generations of his family before him had lived through, "two wars, killer flu, segregation, a nuclear bomb," but then also the things that inspired and amazed them, "the end of two world wars, the polio vaccine, the passage of the civil rights laws. They even saw the Red Sox win the World Series—twice." Josh looked across his family history and saw that the thing his ancestors had in common was fear. Another common thread was hope. He said: "Ever since I was a little kid, whenever I've had a lousy day, my dad would put his arm around me and promise me that 'tomorrow will be a better day.' I challenged my father once, 'How do you know that?' He said, 'I just do.' I believe him. My great-grandparents believe that, and my grandparents, and so do I."

Context can help us look more closely at ideas, at beliefs, and at ourselves. It is the work of powerful readers, yet it is also the work of living an eyes-open life.

I Believe in You
A Vision of Independence

All rituals have a hope, a dream that surrounds them, that transcends the details of the ritual itself: we hold the rites of a wedding for the dream of a happy marriage, we walk the stage at graduation for the dream of success in our chosen careers.

The close reading ritual in this book is no different; its belief is that students leave with the skills to engage deeply with the texts they read, to admire an author's work, and to be critical and passionate readers. Like other rituals, the dream is not really about the rites and steps, instead it is about what it inspires us to achieve. Our hope for your classroom is that at some point your students do not need you to direct them through these steps. As birthday celebrations and "getting ready for school" mornings stack up, rituals become everyday and automatic. The ritual of reading a text closely with a lens, looking for patterns, and then having new understandings is designed so that these structures become ingrained habits, and that these habits then become independent practices for your students.

Hold true to the vision that the end goal is not that students can answer questions about a text only when you ask them, but that they feel inspired to draw on these skills unprompted. Our best teaching is often what helps us fade into the background and allows our students to shine.

Putting It All Together: Allowing a Text to Guide Our Reading

Across the initial chapters of this book we presented close reading skills in lessons that support students in learning, what we call the foundational skills—reading closely for text evidence (Chapter 2), word choice (Chapter 3), and structure (Chapter 4). We then moved to supporting students in combining those skills in Chapters 5 and 6, to read closely to analyze a point of view or argument (Chapter 5) and to make close comparisons between texts (Chapter 6). Now we want to think about the step after that. Specifically, that as students become more developed in reading closely, they can move from deciding ahead of time which lenses to place on a text and instead allow the text to direct them in choosing what to analyze.

To illustrate this, let's move from informational texts and literature, which have been the examples across this book, to look at another genre: poetry. Instead of choosing a lens at first, let's read "Let Go of It," by Cindy Day (1997), and see what lenses the poem invites us to use. Begin by reading through the poem, then we will come back and draw on all of our close reading habits in order to look at it once again, more closely.

Let Go of It

1   *When the wind came up that day*
      I was holding the jib, I was holding it tight
      like Harriet said to and it was something
      to be flying over the bright water,
5   *the wind with us, the shore becoming small,*
      then green, then a dark line.

It was my first time and I was glad
that it was easy, my job steady,
the boat as light as a toy, the water
10   *slipping by with a slipping sound.*

And then the wind changed, turning
like a face in anger, darkly,
and hurled itself at the side of us.
Harriet said, "Let go of it," but I couldn't,
15   *I kept pulling the jib tighter while the mainsail*
she let go of clapped over my head
and the rope tying everything to everything
dug deep into my hands. Disaster is
to me now this perfect symbol,
20   *that boat keeling, Harriet leaning backward*
over starboard, arching her neck as far as it will go
into the wind, the volume of the wind,
the Atlantic spilling in, again
her cry, "Let go of it!" and myself
25   *when I couldn't, when it was more than*
terror, I already believed I was stronger,
bigger than the wind and could not see
how not holding on would save us,
how letting go is holding on.

Reading through once, you probably can't help but have ideas. We think right away, for example: "This poem is about letting go." That feels right, but seemingly great first ideas can become so much better through closer reading. When you go back to reread, know that you can draw on all of the work of this book, pull thinking from across all of the chapters, to develop a new interpretation. To illustrate this, we have described what we were thinking as we reread this poem, and to the left of this we highlighted the skills from this book that we were drawing upon. Notice how we aim to let the poem lead us to different lenses.

considering text evidence

 choose a lens: descriptions and definitions

 choose a lens: techniques as structure

 have a new understanding: a metaphor

 considering point of view

considering text evidence when analyzing point of view

 have a new understanding: what is revealed from these words?

have a new understanding: author's purpose or theme

text evidence

considering text comparisons

have a new understanding: an interpretation by drawing on all lenses

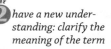 *look for patterns: how do these details fit together?*

have a new understanding: clarify the meaning of the term

considering structure

choose a lens: genre as structure

have a new understanding: what is revealed from these details?

consider word choice when analyzing point of view

considering structure when analyzing point of view

 structure

word choice

consider similarities

consider differences

Let's reread the poem to look more closely at it, drawing on all that we have learned.

Right away in line 2, an **unfamiliar term:** *jib*. But, we know how to handle this! Looking for **descriptions** we can find text evidence such as the *jib* is something you *hold onto tightly*, is related to the *mainsail*, and is the *rope* "tying everything to everything." We notice a **pattern** here: something that holds parts of the boat together. So, **a jib is** either the rope that connects to the sail or a rope in the sail and it needs controlling.

We can reread not with just one lens, but many. Such as noticing a **technique** the poet is using: **repetition**. In lines 2, 15, and 24 the speaker is holding the jib. We ask, "Why would the poet repeat this?" We know that **in poems** often times repeated images connect to meaning. Maybe, **letting go of the jib is like letting go in our lives.**

Feeling more confident, we go back into the poem. It gets us wondering: what exactly **is this poet or poem saying**? To dig into point of view we know we can look more closely at **text evidence**: the storm, the jib, holding on tightly, someone shouting, "Let go of it!" **These seem to** describe a choice: let go or try to control. Then **word choice**: "disaster" in line 18, in line 25 "I couldn't," in line 26 "more than terror," and "I already believed I was stronger, bigger." **This pattern suggests** that trying to control everything might be worse than the storm itself. And then we look to **structure**: the start of the poem is calm, the weather nice, the narrator confident; the end of the poem is dangerous, dark, the narrator uncertain.

We bring all of these together. What is the poet saying about letting go?

We think about **the jib** that controls the sail. **The end of the poem**, in the scariest moment, you are supposed to let go of it. There is also **the phrase**, "letting go is holding on"—but holding onto what? There is a sense that if she lets go, it will be OK. So maybe it is saying we should hold onto trust? Trusting that the boat knows what to do. The sails and the wind will take care of you if you let them.

As we reread we know it helps to think of **other texts in our reading legacy**, comparing them reveals more in both. *The Knife of Never Letting Go* (2008) by Patrick Ness comes to mind, where the characters Todd and Viola struggle so much with trust and survival. **In both** that novel and this poem there is a need to learn to let go—in the poem the jib, and in the book with the world they know. **But these texts are different**, because Todd and Viola feel they must control what is happening around them, they cannot trust life to take care of them. Maybe the poem's narrator fears the same thing? Yet, they learn to rely on one another. Could the poem be saying this as well?

We are now thinking that the poem is saying that there is a time and a place for control—you *should* know how to use a jib to steer a boat—but also sometimes in life you need to let go and trust that you will end up where you need to be. You guided the boat, so the boat can guide you. You supported others, now they can support themselves, support you.

This, then, is a vision to hold in mind during each of the lessons across this book—that our instruction is building toward students' independence, that our ritual becomes their *habit*. Teach the steps so students can use them when they have trouble. Help students develop lenses for looking closely within a text so they will learn to let the text guide them in which lens to use. Guide them to practice ways of finding patterns so they will develop their own strong ideas. The dream of this ritual is that your students will read a text closely on their own, in all of the messy brilliance that entails.

Keeping the Love Alive: Preparing for Your Close Readers

All rituals take some planning. There are the details to arrange: Who is ordering the retirement party cake? How many invitations do we need to print for the sweet sixteen? And then there is the mental preparation: *What tone will I set in my speech? How will I handle the awkwardness of seeing my ex?* For the day to go as planned, someone is performing near magic behind the scenes, ironing the tablecloths, checking the sound system, arranging the flowers. You are that magician for your students, spending your time planning and preparing so they can enter your classroom each day and become even more of themselves than they were just moments ago. The following are some to-dos for your list as you close this book and return to your classroom.

- **Enjoy the bad ideas as much as the great ones.** Sometimes, we learn most from the things that don't go so well at first—a burnt pie, wrong directions, a better-off-without-him breakup. Take the first-draft ideas and the not-so-clear patterns that your students develop as their own current best attempts. Help your students reflect on their learning and give feedback to help them move to the next step, while also celebrating the risks they take when they try. Thinking through how an idea went awry is more important that just knowing a correct response.

- **Talk less, read more.** As we've said before, you only get good at the things you do. Therefore, no matter what we teach, we need to make sure our instruction allows for students to do a lot of independent reading and practice. This may look like having a large part of one period devoted to a lesson, and the next day's period set aside mostly for independent practice. For instance, during a week of reading instruction you might spend two days focusing specifically on close reading skills such as in Figure 7.1.

Mon	Tues	Wed	Thurs	Fri
Your existing reading/writing instruction	Full lesson on close reading for text evidence: LENSES, PATTERNS, IDEAS	A brief reminder of Tuesday's lesson *Then students read and practice independently*	*Your existing reading/writing instruction*	*Your existing reading/writing instruction*

Fig. 7.1 One Scheduling Structure to Allow for Reading and Practice

Another option could be to break a lesson into parts across several days to allow for shorter teaching and more time for students to read each day, such as in the alternate schedule shown in Figure 7.2.

Mon	Tues	Wed	Thurs	Fri
Short lesson on close reading for text evidence: LENSES *Then students read and practice independently*	*Your existing reading/writing instruction*	Short lesson on close reading for text evidence: PATTERNS *Then students read and practice independently*	Short lesson on close reading for text evidence: IDEAS *Then students read and practice independently*	*Your existing reading/writing instruction*

Fig. 7.2 An Alternate Scheduling Structure to Allow for Reading and Practice

Of course, there are several other permutations, including spreading out these shorter lessons across a few weeks.

- **Balance students' reading diet.** Balance the types of texts you read with students and the types of texts they read independently. Think of students developing along two main paths: the complexity of their thinking and the complexity of the texts they can read independently. A novice skier needs to work hard to master skills on the bunny slope with the same attention as an expert skier on a double black diamond. Norman Webb and Karin Hess find that rigor is less about how challenging a text or task is, and more about what knowledge a student draws on to reason deeply (Hess 2004). Across your lessons, vary the genres, levels of challenge, and length of texts. Equally, move freely between analyzing texts, media, and life.

- **Be a vision of reading.** You could simply pretend to care about the lines, the details, the words of a text, and jot down your ideas at the end. This may be just enough. However, if you demonstrate a deep love of language, a fascination with how texts are constructed, and an engagement with building interesting ideas, your students will respond to the texts following your lead.

Unconditional Love: An Endnote

To read something closely is to get to know that text intimately, to hold it close, to cherish its details, to return for more. It is falling in love. It is a ritual for reading and living. At the start of this book, we quoted Socrates: "The unexamined life is not worth living." We believe this to be true. To be truly alive, we need to see and examine what is happening around us, to be aware and responsive and thinking and feeling through it all. We believe that teaching close reading—and teaching in general—is bigger than academics, it is about teaching our students to pay closer attention to life. Close reading skills can help your students to become better, stronger, more detailed readers. But it is also true that teaching your students to read more closely can help them to see themselves and their lives in more vivid detail, with more clarity, full of hope and attention.

All across the country and the world, there are teachers and students who inspire us and exemplify everything that is good and true about our profession. We have found that there are ways of being that the greatest classrooms have in common—mindsets or beliefs that we want to replicate in every school we work with: a love of reading and culture and life, a rigor in looking at texts, and an understanding that all of this reading work has direct parallels to how we live our lives.

We hope this book will help you to tie these things together in your instruction—to be sure that the academics do not consume the love of books and readers, and that the love of books does not prevent us from digging into the deep academic work that we know our students can do.

As you return to your classroom, we challenge you with this: think of not just *how* you will develop a love of living and reading closely, consider how you will pass this love to your students so it lasts. New love can be fickle—if you do not pay it enough attention, or if you worry over it too much, you can drive it away. Whereas deep love—that's developed over time, down valleys and up hills, nurtured with attention and care—is lasting and unconditional. Help your students carry these skills through the school doors and beyond this school year, to the future books they read, the songs they listen to, the conversations they have, and the world they inhabit.

Appendix

Chapter 2

Planning Support for Close Reading:
Possible Lenses, Patterns, Understandings

Text Evidence

	In narratives	*In informational texts*

Types of lenses	• What characters/people: say/ think/do
	• Characters' expressions, gestures, and appearance
	• Relationships
	• Setting descriptions
	• Time period
	• Recurring objects
		A subject's:
		  • Facts
		  • Phrases
		  • Descriptions
		Photos or graphics
		Quotes from experts
		Author's stated opinions
		Comparisons

Types of patterns	• Which details fit together? • How do they fit together?	

Types of understandings	• Character's/people's:
	  ◆ Feelings
	  ◆ Traits
	  ◆ Relationships
	  ◆ Motivations
	  ◆ Comparisons to others
	• Whole text:
	  ◆ Issues
	  ◆ Symbols/metaphors/ motifs
	  ◆ Themes
	  ◆ Lessons
		• Definitions of unknown concepts or terms
		• Main idea of a section
		• Central idea of an entire text
		• Author's bias or point of view
		• Comparisons

Chapter 3

Planning Support for Close Reading:
Possible Lenses, Patterns, Understandings

Word Choice

	In narratives and informational texts

Types of lenses	Choose words that seem particularly selected by the author, such as:
	• Words that evoke:
	    ◆ Strong emotions
	    ◆ Strong images
	    ◆ A clear idea
	• Words that reveal style:
	    ◆ Informal tone
	    ◆ Formal tone
	    ◆ A clear voice
	• Particular kinds of words:
	    ◆ Nouns
	    ◆ Verbs
	    ◆ Adjectives
	    ◆ Adverbs

Types of patterns	• Which words fit together? • How do they fit together?
Types of understandings	An author's: • Tone • Purpose • Relationship to the subject/theme Text's: • Central ideas • Issues • Lessons • Symbols/metaphors/motifs • Themes

Chapter 4

Planning Support for Close Reading:
Possible Lenses, Patterns, Understandings

Structure

	In narratives	In informational texts
Types of lenses	**Lens #1:** Describe the **organization of the text:**	**Lens #1:** Describe the **organization of the text:**
	Genre as structure chosen for a purpose:	*Genre as structure chosen for a purpose:*
	• Fantasy, to explore good and evil • Historical fiction, to reflect on current ideas in a historical context	• Editorial, to convince or persuade • Article, to inform and educate
	Location of parts within the whole:	*Location of parts within the whole:*

	• Plot mountain:
	  ◆ Exposition: introducing character, setting, and backstory
	  ◆ Rising Action: pressures and obstacles
	  ◆ Climax: dramatic point, characters or problems come together
	  ◆ Falling Action: characters or communities change, lessons learned
	  ◆ Resolution: ending, some things wrap up, others might not
		• Sections
		• Text features
		• Order of techniques (see below)

		Techniques the author uses:
	Techniques the author uses:	• Definition of a term • Comparisons • Cause or effect • Description • Anecdote • Claim
	• Descriptions • Dialogue between characters • Action • Setting • Inner thinking • Scene endings and beginning • Flashbacks • Definition of a term • Comparisons	

(continues)

©2014 by Christopher Lehman and Kate Roberts from *Falling in Love with Close Reading: Lessons for Analyzing Texts—and Life*. Portsmouth, NH: Heinemann.

	In narratives	*In informational texts*
Types of lenses *(continued)*	**Lens #2: Purpose** of that organization: • To set the stage • To reveal • To create suspense • To foreshadow	**Lens #2: Purpose** of that organization: • To present a cause for an effect • To make a complex idea more concrete • To provide context • To clear up misconceptions • To develop a reader's expertise
Types of patterns	• How are the parts similar? • How are the parts different? • What purpose do the parts serve?	
Types of understandings	Character: • Development • Changes • Critical moments Whole text: • Themes • Central ideas • Issues • Lessons • Symbols/metaphors/motifs • Author's purpose	• Definitions • Main idea of a section • Central idea of an entire text • Author's bias or point of view • Purpose behind the author's choices

Chapter 5

Planning Support for Close Reading:
Possible Lenses, Patterns, Understandings

Point of View and Argument

	In narratives	*In informational texts*
Types of lenses	**Lens #1:** What is the author's and/or character's point of view here? • What they are thinking • What they believe • What they feel or want **Lens #2:** What makes the author and/or character's point of view persuasive? • Text evidence • Word choice • Structure • What characters: say/think/do • Character expressions, gestures, and appearance • Relationships • Setting descriptions • Time period • Recurring objects	**Lens #1:** What is the point of view/argument? • Ideas or claims • Reasons the claim is right • Evidence supporting the reasons • Counterargument • Logic • Validity • Relevance **Lens #2:** What makes the point of view/argument persuasive? • Text evidence • Word choice • Structure • Emotional appeals (personal stories or anecdotes) • Engaging voice (humor, passion, or outrage) • Sense of audience (angled evidence, or tone) • Nods to commonly held beliefs or even stereotypes • Cacophony, or "ranting" • Rhetorical devices (metaphors, alliteration, or irony)

(continues)

	In narratives	*In informational texts*
Types of patterns	<ul><li>Which points of view/ideas are repeated?</li><li>What technique does the author use to make his or her point of view/argument?</li><li>What sticks out as different or unusual in the text?</li></ul>	
Types of understandings	What is the purpose or effect of these points of view?<ul><li>What is revealed about a theme?</li><li>The author's purpose?</li><li>The effect on the reader?</li><li>Which point of view is rewarded in the text?</li><li>Comparison of points of view</li></ul>	Validity and strength of the argument:<ul><li>Central idea or claim</li><li>Most/least persuasive parts</li><li>How similar or different from the reader's point of view</li><li>How well-supported</li><li>Effective or ineffective parts</li><li>The strength of counterargument</li></ul>Author's style:<ul><li>Most commonly used craft or persuasion techniques</li><li>Balance of style and argument</li><li>Effective or ineffective persuasive techniques</li></ul>

Chapter 6

Planning Support for Close Reading:
Possible Lenses, Patterns, Understandings

Reading Across Texts

Types of lenses	**Lens #1:** Choose a comparison: • Characters or subjects • Themes or central ideas • Settings • Authors (texts by the same author or different author) • Genres • Styles • Other ways (awards won, time period, social issues, etc.) **Lens #2:** Then choose your texts: • What other text fits with this chosen comparison? *Some students may find it helpful to flip these steps.*
Types of patterns	Decide how to compare: • Text evidence • Word choice • Structure • Point of view
Types of understandings	Have new ideas about: • The lens you looked through • The authors' choices • The messages these texts send • See characters or subjects as more complex • Analyze kinds of relationships between characters or ideas in texts • Theme or central idea When considering author's purpose: • Analyze each author's point of view • Understand more of an author's style • See how genre choices affect story, topic, or readers • Examine what it takes to be an "award-winning" book • Analyze what texts from a time period show us about that period in history

References

Alexie, Sherman. 2007. *The Absolutely True Diary of a Part-Time Indian*. New York: Little, Brown and Company.

Allington, Richard L. 2005. *What Really Matters for Struggling Readers: Designing Research-based Programs*. 2nd ed. New York: Longman.

Applegate, Katherine. 2007. *Home of the Brave*. New York: Feiwel and Friends.

———. 2012. *The One and Only Ivan*. New York: Harper.

Arum, Richard, and Josipa Roksa. 2010. *Academically Adrift: Limited Learning on College Campuses*. Chicago, IL: University of Chicago Press.

Atwell, Nancie. 2007. *The Reading Zone: How to Help Kids Become Skilled, Passionate, Habitual, Critical Readers*. New York: Scholastic.

Barnhouse, Dorothy, and Vicki Vinton. 2012. *What Readers Really Do: Teaching the Process of Meaning Making*. Portsmouth, NH: Heinemann.

Beers, Kylene. Twitter Post, April 21, 2011. http://twitter.com/kylenebeers.

Beers, Kylene, and Robert E. Probst. 2012. *Notice and Note: Strategies for Close Reading*. Portsmouth, NH: Heinemann.

Bluedorn, Nathaniel, and Hans Bluedorn. 2005. *The Thinking Toolbox: Thirty-five Lessons That Will Build Your Reasoning Skills*. Muscatine, IA: Christian Logic.

———. 2009. *The Fallacy Detective: Thirty-eight Lessons on How to Recognize Bad Reasoning*. Muscatine, IA: Christian Logic.

Bomer, Randy, and Katherine Bomer. 2001. *For a Better World: Reading and Writing for Social Action*. Portsmouth, NH: Heinemann.

Bransford, John D., Ann L. Brown, and Rodney R. Cocking, et al. eds. 2000. *How People Learn: Brain, Mind, Experience, and School*. Expanded Edition. Washington, DC: National Academy Press.

Bronner, Kristopher. 2013. "How to Change the World." TEDx Teen: The Audacity of whY video. We Are Family Foundation. www.tedxteen.com/talks/tedxteen-2013/165-kristopher-bronner-how-to-change-the-world.

Brontë, Charlotte. (1847) 1991. *Jane Eyre*. New York: Knopf.

Brown, Margaret Wise. 1947. *Goodnight Moon*. New York: HarperCollins.

Burke, Jim. 2012. *The English Teacher's Companion: A Completely New Guide to Classroom, Curriculum, and the Profession*. Portsmouth, NH: Heinemann.

Calkins, Lucy. 2001. *The Art of Teaching Reading*. New York: Longman.

Calkins, Lucy, and Kathleen Tolan. 2010. *Navigating Nonfiction*. Portsmouth, NH: Heinemann.

Calkins, Lucy, Kathleen Tolan, and Mary Ehrenworth. 2010. *Units of Study for Teaching Reading, Grades 3–5: A Curriculum for the Reading Workshop*. Portsmouth, NH: Heinemann.

Calkins, Lucy, Mary Ehrenworth, and Christopher Lehman. 2012. *Pathways to the Common Core: Accelerating Achievement*. Portsmouth, NH: Heinemann

Carle, Eric. 1979. *The Very Hungry Caterpillar*. New York: Collins.

Clark, Roy Peter. 2006. *Writing Tools: 50 Essential Strategies for Every Writer*. New York: Little, Brown and Company.

Coleman, David, and Susan Pimentel. 2012. "Revised Publishers' Criteria for the Common Core State Standards in English Language Arts and Literacy, Grades 3–12." www.corestandards.org/assets/Publishers_Criteria_for_3-12.pdf.

Collins, Suzanne. 2008. *The Hunger Games*. New York: Scholastic.

David, Laurie, and Cambria Gordon. 2007. *The Down-to-Earth Guide to Global Warming*. New York: Orchard Books.

Day, Cindy. 1997. "Let Go of It." In *Last Call: Poems on Alcoholism, Addiction, and Deliverance*, edited by Sarah Gorham and Jeffrey Skinner. Louisville, KY: Sarabande Books.

Dickens, Charles. 1859. *A Tale of Two Cities*. London: Chapman & Hall.

Draper, Sharon M. 2012. *Out of My Mind*. New York: Atheneum Books for Young Readers.

Duke, Nell K., and P. D. Pearson. 2002. "Effective Practices for Developing Reading Comprehension," in *What Research Has to Say About Reading Instruction*. 3rd ed. International Reading Association.

Epstein, Norman, and Donald H. Baucom. 2002. *Enhanced Cognitive-behavioral Therapy for Couples: A Contextual Approach*. Washington, DC: American Psychological Association.

Fish, Stanley. 1970. "Literature in the Reader: Affective Stylistics." *New Literary History* 2 (1): 123–162. The Johns Hopkins University Press.

Fisher, Douglas. "Douglas Fisher: Close Reading and the Common Core State Standards, Part 1." School Education Group video, 2:47. Posted April 2012. www.youtube.com/watch?v=5w9v6-zUg3Y.

Fisher, Douglas, and Nancy Frey. 2012. *Text Complexity and Close Readings*. Newark, DE: International Reading Association.

Fisher, Douglas, Nancy Frey, and Diane Lapp. 2012. *Text Complexity: Raising Rigor in Reading*. Newark, DE: International Reading Association.

Gallagher, Kelly. 2004. *Deeper Reading: Comprehending Challenging Texts, 4–12*. Portland, ME: Stenhouse Publishers.

Gantos, Jack. (1998) 2011. *Joey Pigza Swallowed the Key*. New York: Square Fish.

Graff, Gerald, and Cathy Birkenstein. 2007. *They Say / I Say: The Moves That Matter in Academic Writing*. New York: W. W. Norton & Company.

Green, John. 2012. *The Fault in Our Stars*. New York: Dutton Books.

Harvey, Paul. 1978. "So God Made a Farmer." Speech at Future Farmers of America Convention.

Harvey, Stephanie, and Anne Goudvis. 2000. *Strategies That Work: Teaching Comprehension to Enhance Understanding*. Portland, ME: Stenhouse Publishers.

Hattie, John. 2008. *Visible Learning: A Synthesis of Over 800 Meta-Analyses Relating to Achievement*. London: Routledge.

———. 2012. *Visible Learning for Teachers: Maximizing Impact on Learning*. London: Routledge.

Hawthorne, Nathaniel. (1843) 1987. "The Birthmark." In *Nathaniel Hawthorne's Tales (Norton Critical Editions)*, edited by James McIntosh. New York: W. W. Norton & Company.

Hess, Karin K. 2004. "Applying Webb's Depth-of-Knowledge (DOK) Levels in Reading." Dover, NH: National Center for Assessment. http://bllblogs.typepad.com/files/dokreading_kh08.pdf.

———. 2008. "Teaching and Assessing Understanding of Text Structures Across Grades." National Center for the Improvement of Educational Assessment. www.nciea.org/publications/TextStructures_KH08.pdf.

Horowitz, Anthony. 2007. *Nightrise*. New York: Scholastic Press.

Howe, James, ed. 2006. *13: Thirteen Stories That Capture the Agony and Ecstasy of Being Thirteen*. New York: Atheneum Books for Young Readers.

Hurst, James, and Philippe Dumas. 1988. *The Scarlet Ibis*. Mankato, MN: Creative Education.

Johnson, Angela. 2003. *The First Part Last*. New York: Simon & Schuster Books for Young Readers.

Kain, Patricia. 1998. "How to Do a Close Reading." Writing Center at Harvard University. www.fas.harvard.edu/~wricntr/documents/CloseReading.html.

Keene, Ellin Oliver. 2012. *Talk About Understanding: Rethinking Classroom Talk to Enhance Comprehension*. Portsmouth, NH: Heinemann.

Kisbert-Smith, Amber. 2013. "Middle School Challenges Students, Staff to Go 'Screen Free.'" *Pierce County Herald*. April 24, 2013. www.piercecountyherald.com/event/article/id/52745/group/News/.

Kittle, Penny. 2012. *Book Love: Developing Depth, Stamina, and Passion in Adolescent Readers*. Portsmouth, NH: Heinemann.

Langer, Judith A. 2001. "Beating the Odds: Teaching Middle and High School Students to Read and Write Well." *American Educational Research Journal* 38 (4) 837–880. doi:10.3102/00028312038004837.

Lee, Harper. 1960. *To Kill a Mockingbird*. Philadelphia: Lippincott.

Lehman, Christopher. 2012. *Energize Research Reading and Writing: Fresh Strategies to Spark Interest, Develop Independence, and Meet Key Common Core Standards, Grades 4–8*. Portsmouth, NH: Heinemann.

Levin, Samuel R. 1998. *Shades of Meaning: Reflections on the Use, Misuse, and Abuse of English*. Boulder, CO: Westview Press.

Lowry, Lois. 1993. *The Giver*. Boston, MA: Houghton Mifflin.

———. 2009. *Crow Call*. New York: Scholastic Press.

Marzano, Robert J. 2007. *The Art and Science of Teaching: A Comprehensive Framework for Effective Instruction*. Alexandria, VA: ASCD.

Marzano, Robert J., Debra J. Pickering, and Jane E. Pollock. 2001. *Classroom Instruction That Works: Research-based Strategies for Increasing Student Achievement*. Alexandria, VA: ASCD.

Mascarelli, Amanda Leigh. 2013. "Fooling the Mind's Eye." *Science News for Kids*. www.sciencenewsforkids.org/2012/09/brain-scientists-learn-from-magicians-and-their-tricks/.

Meyer, Stephenie. 2005. *Twilight*. New York: Little, Brown and Company.

Miller, Donalyn. 2009. *The Book Whisperer: Awakening the Inner Reader in Every Child*. San Francisco, CA: Jossey-Bass.

Mooney, Margaret E. 1990. *Reading to, with, and by Children*. Katonah, NY: Richard C. Owen Publishers.

Myers, Walter Dean. 2007. *What They Found: Love on 145th Street*. New York: Wendy Lamb Books.

National Governors Association Center for Best Practices, Council of Chief State School Officers. 2010. *English Language Arts Standards*. Common Core State Standards Initiative. www.corestandards.org/ELA-Literacy.

Nemours Foundation. 2011. "Hand Washing." TeensHealth.org. http://teenshealth.org/teen/your_body/skin_stuff/handwashing.html.

Nerdy Book Club Blog; "Canon Fodder," blog entry by Donalyn Miller, March 11, 2013. http://nerdybookclub.wordpress.com/2013/03/11/canon-fodder-by-donalyn-miller/.

Ness, Patrick. 2008. *The Knife of Never Letting Go*. Cambridge, MA: Candlewick Press.

Newkirk, Thomas. 2012. *The Art of Slow Reading: Six Time-honored Practices for Engagement*. Portsmouth, NH: Heinemann.

Nye, Naomi Shihab. 2011. *There Is No Long Distance Now: Very Short Stories*. New York: Greenwillow Books.

Palacio, R. J. 2012. *Wonder*. New York: Alfred A. Knopf.

Parker, Kathleen. 2012. "Digital Books Leave a Reader Cold." *Washington Post*. http://articles.washingtonpost.com/2012-12-28/opinions/36071843_1_digital-books-print-edition-smell.

Pearson, P. David. 2011. "Toward the Next Generation of Comprehension Instruction." *Comprehension Going Forward*. Portsmouth, NH: Heinemann.

Pearson, P. David, and M. C. Gallagher. 1983. "The Instruction of Reading Comprehension." *Contemporary Educational Psychology* 8: 317–344.

Ransom, John Crowe. 1941. *The New Criticism*. Norfolk, CT: New Directions Publishing Corporation.

Ray, Katie Wood. 1999. *Wondrous Words: Writers and Writing in the Elementary Classroom*. Urbana, IL: National Council of Teachers of English.

Reilly, Rick. 1999. "Sis! Boom! Bah! Humbug!" http://sportsillustrated.cnn.com/vault/article/magazine/MAG1017375/.

Rittenberg, Josh. 2006. "Tomorrow Will Be a Better Day." *Morning Edition*, NPR. www.npr.org/templates/story/story.php?storyId=5232116.

Rosenblatt, Louise M. 1938. *Literature as Exploration*. D. Appleton-Century Company, Inc.

———. 1978. *The Reader, the Text, the Poem: The Transactional Theory of the Literary Work*. Carbondale, IL: Southern Illinois University Press.

Rowling, J. K. 1999. *Harry Potter and the Sorcerer's Stone*. New York: Scholastic.

Santman, Donna. 2005. *Shades of Meaning: Comprehension and Interpretation in Middle School*. Portsmouth, NH: Heinemann.

Scieszka, Jon, ed. 2005. *Guys Write for Guys Read*. New York: Viking.

Seavert, Lindsey. 2012. "Teen Creates Viral Campaign to Stop Cyberbullies." *USA Today*.

Serravallo, Jennifer. 2010. *Teaching Reading in Small Groups: Differentiated Instruction for Building Strategic, Independent Readers*. Portsmouth, NH: Heinemann.

Shanahan, Timothy. 2013. "The Common Core Ate My Baby and Other Urban Legends." www.ascd.org/publications/educational-leadership/dec12/vol70/num04/The-Common-Core-Ate-My-Baby-and-Other-Urban-Legends.aspx.

Shetty, Baba, and Tina Brown. 2012. "A Turn of the Page for Newsweek." *The Daily Beast*. www.thedailybeast.com/articles/2012/10/18/a-turn-of-the-page-for-newsweek.html.

Smith, Crystal. 2011. "Word Cloud: How Toy Ad Vocabulary Reinforces Gender Stereotypes." The Achilles Effect. www.achilleseffect.com/2011/03 word-cloud-how-toy-ad-vocabulary-reinforces-gender-stereotypes/.

Smith, Michael W., and Jeffrey D. Wilhelm. 2002. *Reading Don't Fix No Chevys: Literacy in the Lives of Young Men*. Portsmouth, NH: Heinemann.

Spinelli, Jerry. 2000. *Stargirl*. New York: Knopf.

Steinbeck, John. (1937) 1986. *Of Mice and Men*. New York: Viking.

Tatum, Alfred W. 2009. *Reading for Their Life: (Re)building the Textual Lineages of African American Adolescent Males*. Portsmouth, NH: Heinemann.

Tovani, Cris. 2004. *Do I Really Have to Teach Reading? Content Comprehension, Grades 6–12*. Portland, ME: Stenhouse Publishers.

Veeser, H. Aram. 1989. *The New Historicism*. New York: Routledge.

Vygotsky, Lev. 1978. "Interaction Between Learning and Development." *Mind and Society* 79–91. Cambridge, MA: Harvard University Press.

West, Kasie. 2013. *Pivot Point*. New York: HarperTeen.

Wild, Margaret, and Ron Brooks. 2006. *Fox*. La Jolla, CA: Kane/Miller Book Publishers.

Wiles, Deborah. 2001. *Freedom Summer*. New York: Atheneum Books for Young Readers.

Wimsatt, Jr. W. K., ed. 1954. *The Verbal Icon: Studies in the Meaning of Poetry*. Lexington, KT: University of Kentucky.

Wimsatt, Jr., W. K., and Monroe C. Beardsley. 1946. "The Intentional Fallacy." *The Sewanee Review* 54 (3): 468–488. Baltimore, MD: The Johns Hopkins University Press.

———. 1949. "The Affective Fallacy." *The Sewanee Review* 57 (1): 31–55. Baltimore, MD: The Johns Hopkins University Press.

XPLANE, The Economist, Karl Fisch, Scott McLeod, and Laura Bestler. 2009. "Did You Know 4.0." Posted September 2009. www.youtube.com/watch?v=6ILQrUrEWe8.

TRANSFORM YOUR STUDENTS INTO ENGAGED AND INDEPENDENT RESEARCHERS

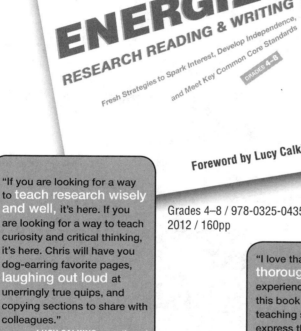

Christopher Lehman

ENERGIZE
RESEARCH READING & WRITING

Fresh Strategies to Spark Interest, Develop Independence, and Meet Key Common Core Standards

GRADES 4–8

Foreword by Lucy Calkins

Grades 4–8 / 978-0325-04357-9
2012 / 160pp

Heinemann
DEDICATED TO TEACHERS

WEB **Heinemann.com**
CALL **800.225.5800** • FAX **877.231.6980**

@HeinemannPub